SEVEN STEPS TO IMPROVE YOUR PEOPLE SKILLS

NEIL MULLARKEY

First published in the United Kingdom in 2017 by
London Business Forum
38 Bartholomew Close
London
EC1A 7HP
www.londonbusinessforum.com

Cover and text design by Howdy
Typeset by PJ Crittenden

Produced for London Business Forum by Essential Works
www.essentialworks.co.uk

ISBN: 978-0993501128

CONTENTS

Acknowledgements

I owe a huge debt of gratitude to all of the people who have attended my workshops over the last 18 years. We've had fun and I have learned so much. I am especially grateful to those whom I have coached one-on-one. It is a privilege to be able to spend time with someone and learn their story.

Many thanks to the following:

- Lucy Anstie, my editor, who has been so diligent and encouraging along the way. She's been firm but fair.
- Brendan Barns, founder of the London Business Forum, not only for publishing this book, but for giving me the chance to see all those great speakers over the years who have inspired and educated me. Thanks to Katie and Amelia too.
- Simon Dane, Clive Holtham, Gillian King and Nicola Phillips for reading the manuscript late in the day. I didn't give you the chance to change much so you cannot be blamed.
- The Comedy Store Players for making me laugh week in, week out for over three decades, and for allowing me to play with them.
- To my wife and children. You know how my people skills desert me every day, yet you forgive me. I do love you so very much.

This book is for my Dad, who is no longer with us. He was the first businessman I met. He took none of it too seriously.

STEPPIN' OUT

Maybe you've picked this book up by mistake and are hoping to put it back down soon. You've been told you're not a 'people person' or you don't feel you want to be one.
You might be thinking one of three things:

1. 'I'm an introvert. This is all about being outgoing.'
2. 'My job is technical. All this people stuff is irrelevant.'
3. 'Oh just leave me alone!'

Unsurprisingly, I have an answer for each.

1. So many great leaders and communicators are actually introverts. Susan Cain's great book, *Quiet: The Power of Introverts in a World That Can't Stop Talking*, makes the case for understanding and cherishing those who would not naturally consider themselves extroverts. No matter what kind of person you are, you can pick up and practise the skills necessary so as not to be drowned out.

2. If I am too good at people skills, my technical skills will be overlooked'... SAID NOBODY EVER. Whatever your 'hard' skills are, improving your soft skills will only help them come to the fore.

3. You don't have to be 'on' 24/7. Amy Cuddy, the brilliant Harvard psychology professor (and Queen of TED Talks), wrote a book called *Presence*. When I saw her speak at the London Business Forum, she admitted that it's okay if you're not always 'present'. There will be times when you just want to chill or keep your head down. Fine. All the more reason that when you ARE in non-chill mode, you consciously manage your impact and step up to the plate.

Technological disruption and automation are changing the job landscape, but this means people skills are going to become MORE urgent not less. It will be all the more important to be able to communicate, collaborate, cope with complexity, adapt to new ways of working, delegate, deal with ambiguity, influence, empathise, share power, give and receive feedback and understand what motivates others.

I asked my friend, Simon Dane, Head of Leadership & Talent at PA Consulting, what he thought was the basis of good people skills. Without a breath, he replied, 'be curious, be confident'. Brilliant. So applicable with people you've just met or with those you see every day.

In this book I am going to suggest Seven Steps for improving your people skills. And they all begin with L.

However, just because you have picked up (and hopefully now bought) this book does not mean that anything will change. You need to notice the anxieties you may have around your social skills and see how they may be holding you back. Perhaps you've not seen the point of working on these things, that these are just a 'given'. But you can improve and my first step, Learn, will even help you to develop the ways you learn.

My aim is to encourage you to think and act so that your time in organisations, large or small, may be just a little easier, a bit more effective. Why shouldn't you be able to communicate the best version of yourself more regularly?

You may even find yourself Steppin' Out of your comfort zone.

Along the way I will highlight some Simple Steps in blue letters like this. Snazzy, huh?

I often find that failures with people issues are costing organisations so much time, money and energy. Emmanuel Gobillot, consultant and author, wisely tells his clients that they are very happy to set targets for 'hard' business outcomes with numbers and so forth, so why not set such goals for 'soft' skills? Can you improve a certain amount in a certain time?

Just one percent would be good, wouldn't it? That's how the British Cycling Team became so good. The aggregation of marginal gains means that you try and improve each area by just one percent. Put them together and gold medals are within reach.

How about we aim for seven per cent, one for each of the steps?

Footnotes

Originally I wasn't going to have any footnotes, preferring to put clear details in the text if people wanted to follow up. I don't know about you but, as a reader, I am always torn. When I see a little number

I feel I should go and check the reference but I kind of want to carry on and not lose the flow. But then, if I do look later at the footnotes I can't remember what they referred to. So I have done footnotes but not too many. There isn't a footnote for every reference I make. And they are there to give you the option to read further if you want to.

Professor Clive Holtham (of City University and one of my early champions when I was making the move into management training, and whose continuing support and advice I cherish) said this book should be on the reading list for business schools, where students would want more footnotes. Oh, all right then.

I have cited plenty of scientific research but some of that has and will continue to be challenged. Were the samples big enough? Can it be replicated? Is the professor a rotter? Psychological tests in lab conditions are not real life. Later, I will urge you to start collecting your own data. Try things out.

STEP ONE
LEARN

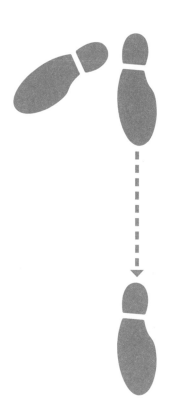

In this book, I will draw on my experience in the theatre, on the stage, and often specifically as an improv performer. Isn't life an improvisation after all?

In improv, we often talk about what the character learns in a scene. How are they altered by the interaction with another? I wonder how things would be if we thought about our conversations and interactions in this way? What have we learned? Can we be altered, even in a tiny way? If that were your mindset how would you approach your conversations differently?

This is why I particularly like how my friend, Simon Dane, characterises people skills as being about curiosity and confidence.

> What can you learn about this person?
> What can you learn from this person?
> What can s/he learn from you?

Every person has a story. You can learn something from everybody. Even if it's how not to do things. But take some time to analyse why that is not the way you would do things. Or how you would do things if you were the other person.

Are you yearnin' for learnin'?

You may have heard of the Myers-Briggs personality tests. It's all splendid stuff. You answer questions about how, for example, you make decisions or whether you are more inwardly or outwardly focused. This helps determine your personality type, expressed in four letters, which show your preferences. I have seen it brilliantly applied to help people understand a little more about themselves.

Trouble is, there is no science behind it and I have also seen it lazily rolled out as a reason for why people cannot change because they have been labelled…

'Oh I'm an ENTJ. It's how I am. I always [insert unforgivable behaviour]'

'Don't ask me, I'm an ISTP. I don't do [insert perfectly reasonable thinking]'

If you are not careful it's as easy and glib as saying, 'Oh that's not my style, dahling, I'm a Taurus.'

However, I mention it because it is about preferences and acknowledges that we are all different. 'This is the way I do things, but that's the way you do things'. That seems a reasonable starting point.

I observed the leadership team of a financial services firm being led through their Myers-Briggs profiles. It was fascinating to see the CEO admit that he didn't listen much to praise but was always looking for criticism to help him put things right. The marketing person happily revealed she needed about eight pieces of positive feedback, even on the smallest of things, before she could face anything negative.

When these personality models are effective, they make you pause before responding to others, and make you notice where you should pay attention to your own behaviour.

Think of yourself as a work-in-progress.

> 'I never lose. I either win or learn.'
> Nelson Mandela

Although it doesn't always feel like that, does it? Sometimes, it just feels like you lost. You made a total mess of things.

I often remember, with a shudder, moments when I said the wrong thing, long ago. Then I recall a ghastly boo-boo I made only last week. At my age I really should know better. But if we can make these ups and downs into a story, we can feel stronger. And there is even evidence that the stories parents tell of their own past (good and bad) affect the resilience of their children. There are two ways of telling stories:

1. Bad things happen, therefore the world is bad.
2. Bad things happen, but I still managed to carry on.

Telling a story, making the utter hash we made of things into an amusing anecdote, can render it enabling rather than toxic. It can be helpful to any group and any individual. It helps us make sense of where we are and where we might go.

As a parent, I have encountered a lot of research into learning which has really helped me understand more about my own work and attitudes. Perhaps you have heard of 'growth mindset', a term coined by the American educationalist, Carol Dweck. She set ten-year-old children tasks that she knew would be slightly too difficult.

One group said things like, 'I love a challenge', and were thinking about what they could learn from the experience. For Dweck, they had a growth mindset. For others, it was disaster. They had what she calls a fixed mindset. Asked what they might do next time, they said they would cheat or locate someone who did worse than them to make themselves feel better by comparison. They ran away from the problem.

Researchers even looked at the electrical activity in their brains when faced with an error. There wasn't much for the fixed group. As for the growth group, there was plenty. For them, abilities can be enhanced by engaging with a challenge. They process an error. They learn from it and they correct it. For the fixed group, they felt their intelligence was being judged. Finding things difficult and having to make an effort made them feel foolish.

It's an attitude to learning. Fixed mindset says, 'I'm good at this'. When you come up against a problem you lose confidence.

Growth mindset says, 'I can learn to be good at this'. You become better at something because you worked at it. So not being good at something now does not mean you won't be good at it later. Our brains are very plastic, not just in early life, so we can continue to learn.

Think of that as you ponder these pages. You can improve. You may not be brilliant at some of it yet. You can try things out. I have seen plenty of people improve, even in a few hours, whatever their starting point.

How to improve the way you learn

In theatre, we rehearse. We have lines and try them out in different ways; fast or slow, loud or quiet, pausing here or there. (Actually, there may be more to it than that, but you get my drift.)

We are prepared for some ideas not to work and yet sometimes it is these ideas which hit just the right note. This is the importance of putting things on their feet. You can't really tell until you've had a go. There are lots of business areas in which this 'rapid prototyping' has become the norm, like Design Thinking and Agile. It's about trying things out early.

Babies love to learn. They experiment, using their bodies to find out what things are like. Sadly, once they are able to compare themselves with others, learning can take a back seat to performance. It becomes about being the best.

Herminia Ibarra, a proper professor at a top business school, has written a book called *Act Like a Leader, Think Like a Leader*. Read that title again. Note the order. You can act your way into a new way of thinking.

I find that people are uneasy about trying things out because it's somehow not authentic. Surely being authentic doesn't mean failing to change or to learn new skills? It does mean having values but you can adapt your style to different situations. 'The trick is to work towards a future version of your authentic self', says Herminia.

When I became a father I had to become a new version of myself. It wasn't just about learning to change nappies. You have to make choices on boundaries, on what you choose to say, on how you talk about other people...

It's not about being an imposter but stretching yourself. Herminia quotes psychologist Mark Snyder, who talks about 'chameleons' and 'true-to-selfers'. Chameleon sounds bad or fake, doesn't it? No. They are no less value-driven. They have simply learnt to adapt their style to different situations.

True-to-selfers may include their style, clothes and demeanour in the picture of who they really are. 'I'm very much a take me as you find me person', is how the supposedly blunt British say it. (A bit like Myers-Briggs fundamentalists?)

But what if I 'find' you when you've just won the lottery or when you've come out of a bad job interview or when you're on holiday? Will you be the same? And, vitally, it's not just how you are but how I am that affects how I 'find' you.

Many true-to-selfers are good or even great at the technical tasks required by their job yet aren't interested in exploring the rest that may be required ... the people skills that characterise leadership.

Herminia talks about being able to play. That's a much better approach. Try things out with no need to commit. She cites psychologist Tory Higgins who talks about 'promotion orientation' versus 'prevention orientation'. One is about experimenting to find new ways, one is reducing ways of going wrong.

I see this when encouraging people to rehearse their presentations. Some are not keen. Instead of seeing rehearsal as a chance to improve, they fear being exposed if they are not very good. But only by rehearsing can they become better.

I used to wonder whether it was laziness or fear. After eighteen years, I am convinced it is fear. I have seen plenty who are willing to give it a go and have been rewarded. They are ready to learn the art of rehearsal. Actually, it is more of a science, in that a series of continuing experiments lead to observations which lead to results and then conclusions and eventually changed behaviour (not necessarily in that order).

In 1984, David Kolb put forward a theory of learning. It's a cycle...
- Do something
- Reflect on what you did
- Make generalisations based on your reflections
- Plan what you'll do next time

Then back to...
- Do something ... and so on...

In improv, we do workshops. We look back at a scene and think about the choices we made. Or a director can step in and suggest a tweak before the scene continues, to see where it might lead.

How to learn someone's name
The first thing you learn when you meet someone is their name. Except you might not try to learn it. You might let it waft over, like a pleasant smell of baking muffins.

I run full day workshops and give conference speeches to hundreds of people, often all some participants want to know is how I remember names.

It's simple.

I really want to learn their names

When I was little, I felt an immediate disconnect from grown-ups who did not observe this common courtesy. If your name is Nigel or Neville, do not be offended but please understand how much a little boy called Neil would not want to be addressed thus.

So that's the psychological imperative. Next, I cheat. No, I rehearse.

I always ask for a list of names ahead of an event. Who will be in my workshop? I look for first names that I might find hard to pronounce or where there are two people with the same name.

Ask for names ahead of time
Plant a seed in your memory
Start the rehearsal

You can do this if you have a meeting, a pitch or a job interview. Familiarise yourself with those names. If you aren't sure how to pronounce one, ring up and ask. It's perfectly acceptable. Who wouldn't want to help you in this way? Who wouldn't be pleased that you are making extra efforts?

Take a few minutes to write down those names. Yes, write them down in long hand. My son's primary school teacher told me that we remember things better if we have written them down, even more than typing or saying them.

Then I read an article in *The Economist* citing studies which showed that students remembered more if writing long hand.[1] Those who typed on a device made more notes but didn't recall as much information. Writing long hand means not writing everything down but choosing what to write and making connections, which helps plant the knowledge.

Richard Branson writes things down so he can remember them, whether it's a good idea or a number that comes up in negotiation.

Road Dahl wrote down little ideas which he revisited many years later. So buy a notebook. Write things down. Ideas, things you notice, or people you could contact.

Anyway, back to names...

Before participants arrive for the workshop, I write their names down on a flip chart, which they see as they enter (and they always check to see if their own name is there!) I tick off each name as I meet its owner.

I greet people one at a time. More than three in one go is impossible. I meet the person, ask their name, repeat it as I look at them, look away and say it in my head then look back at them, then go and tick off their name on the chart.

Write down names

Say them out loud

Say them in your head

You can do the same, as discreetly as you like. You can tick them off your list. So now I have:

1. A picture of the person in my mind.
2. The sound of their name.
3. A picture of their name and all those letters in the right order.

After about half a dozen people have arrived, I discreetly step away and (in my head) say each person's name quietly as I look at them, to cement the connection.

Round a table it's useful to draw a little map, with an X for each name indicating where people are sitting.

This may all sound very obvious. It certainly is. You may do one or more of these already. However, I have found plenty of people who do not and they have given up. They're delighted by these easy tips.

I encounter many people who tell me they are terrible with names. Don't say that. Start afresh. Like everything in this book ...

You can learn to learn

It's acceptable to ask again a bit later if none of the above has made a name stick. But not years later, ideally within in the first ten minutes. Even better if you can ally their name with another mental image (such as something about their journey today or other snippet you can find in 'small talk').

I was told about someone whose name is also Neil who, when helping people learn it, got down on one knee. 'See, it's Neil as in Kneel.'

For some encounters, you may have to accept that you are putting their name in your Flash Drive, not your Hard Drive. It's a memory stick and it could get wiped or lost. So it might make it easier if you just think, 'I only have to remember their names today'.

Of course, it is a good idea if you can transfer that memory stick to your database. I try and follow up with an email or a LinkedIn invitation. I print out and file every list of participants (yes, I have very large shelves). Often I put a note next to each person such as a hobby or place they've mentioned or something (or someone) we have in common. It's amazing how, when you run a small business based almost entirely on recommendations, those names reappear years later.

Simple Steps for learning names

- Request a list of names ahead of a meeting.

- Make sure that you hear each name individually.

- Give good eye contact when you hear a name and when you then repeat it.

- Go slowly. Don't move on to the next person until you feel you've really nailed the current name in your head.

- Write down names to cement the connection.

Learning curve?

If you know who is going to be in a meeting, look them up, perhaps on LinkedIn rather than anything more personal. You don't want to be too creepy ... 'Ooh I see you have three children, that you shopped at Sainsbury's on Saturday and you like walnut whips.'

Just try and discover something you may have in common, or something about them that you find especially interesting. They will take it as a compliment that you took the trouble.

Once you have learned someone's name, it's time to learn what makes them tick. They may be very different from you. They may be very different from anyone else you've ever met.

People are wired differently, in terms of what motivates them, de-motivates them and annoys them. We each have a different story. Actually, we all have a whole lot of different stories we tell ourselves and others. Do you think Myers-Briggs were right to say that there are only sixteen personality types?

> 'Every individual is an exception to the rule.'
> Carl Jung

It all starts with L

When I created my Seven Steps, Learn was just for learning people's names and learning what you can about them but I have come to see that learning underpins the other six.

I read once that you can learn only when you realise that you don't know something, so every act of learning involves a blow to the self-esteem because it means that you weren't perfect before.

I frequently meet people who are very experienced and accomplished but with a little digging, I find they are latching onto a comment from way back and still use it to punish themselves...

'I've been told I giggle too much'
'I've been told I talk too quickly'
'I've been told I talk in a monotone'

They have held this information in the ledger of debits rather than working to turn it into a credit. Sometimes it becomes much bigger than the feedback itself ...

'I am no good at communicating'
'I can't improve at this social stuff'
'I'm just a technical person'

Just as comedians will notice the one person who is not laughing as they entertain a packed and roaring theatre, people often hold onto the negative moments.

But you need to notice these anxieties in order to learn.

It's also important to have the right emotional parameters. You've got to care about this and it's got to be enjoyable when you put it into practice, maybe even fun. Make a game of it, whether it be noticing others' people skills or trying a thing out on a Friday afternoon, just to see ...

You might be able to recall some of the things I write here. You might like the quotes from famous people and maybe even remember some of the Simple Steps, but unless you emotionally commit to do something about it, to really learn, which means rehearsing, observing role models, and trying things out, then I won't have been much use to you (see, I can play hard cop as well as soft cop).

> 'You must begin to think of yourself as becoming the person you want to be.'
> David Viscott

Simple Steps

- Decide to adopt a growth mindset. Even your boo-boos can become great stories.

- Experiment. Play. Don't be scared to be a chameleon.

- Mimic and observe the impact (on yourself and others).

- You may need to make mistakes in public to really learn so take on a coach or do a course. Not sure what kind of course? Try improv, where even failure is fun:

- Buy a notebook to help you recall what worked.

STEP TWO
LOOK

When I was young, there was really only one talk show on British TV, hosted by Michael Parkinson. The guests that most people remember are Muhammad Ali and Billy Connolly but I found another person utterly captivating. His name is Desmond Morris. He applied his zoologist training to the study of human beings. His book, *Manwatching*, introduced the concept of body language to many. He explained how we use our hands, our face, our torso and more, to show, or sometimes fail to hide, our true intent.

Seared into my memory is the graphic he showed of where our gaze is directed when we look at another person. It flits between each of the eyes, occasionally checking out the nose, the mouth, or other parts of the body. But the eyes have it.

Lookin' good?

I notice that a lot of people do not give quality eye contact. A few months ago, someone I know was trying to convince another person of her idea. But she kept looking at me, whom she knows better, rather than at him. Perhaps she was nervous of being rejected and regarded me as a safe pair of eyes. I experimented by pointing her in the direction of the other person (without him noticing) as if to say, 'Not me, look at him! He's the one who needs convincing!' I did it three times in as many minutes and still her eyes came back to me. Her idea has not been implemented.

You can change your eye contact techniques fairly easily and more readily than your voice, your posture or your clothes (other aspects of self-presentation upon which others might make snap judgments).

When you meet someone for the first time, you need to show that you are curious and confident. Eye contact achieves both.

Bill Clinton is famous for giving great eye contact, especially when he is introduced to someone new. Apparently he even looks back at you when he is moved on to the next person.

Eye contact means attention. We give plenty away with our eyes. From an evolutionary psychology point of view, that's a good thing because we can know how others feel. That is useful for both parties. The eyes readily convey anger, fear and surprise. This would have been very helpful for cavemen and cavewomen when faced with a situation that needed rapid communication. With just a quick change of facial expression, they could convey those three emotions, in silence...

... watch out for the sabre tooth tiger.

... look at the nice fruit I have found on this tree.

... I would like to procreate with you.

How to improve your eye contact

Eye contact is something of a dance. Keep the same rhythm as the person or persons around you. Don't try to cha-cha-cha if others are fox-trotting (or something, I don't know much about proper dancing.) Maybe you shouldn't try pogoing if the other person is doing a pas de deux?

The fun is that you can practise eye contact technique at any time with anyone, whether you know them or not.

Try increasing pleasant, appropriate eye
contact with shop assistants, waiters and
hotel staff – by just one moment.*

A moment is of variable length, depending on the context.

Don't hold it too long. See how long too long is. Michael Ellsberg, in his brilliant book *The Power of Eye Contact*, suggests you do it while walking through town.[1] Try and look at people you pass just long enough to see the colour of their eyes, then look away. Look away to the side, not down. How you break eye contact is important as well. Not too fast, not too slow. Keep a neutral expression or a slight smile if you like. See how people react. You may well receive a smile in return.

In my workshops, I ask people to play a game where they deliberately break eye contact in conversation with another. It's very off-putting. As a game it's fun but people notice how it matters in real life. Then I ask them to look for too long. Surprisingly, they find this harder. Somehow they find it easier to be off-hand than to gaze a little longer at someone, even when socially sanctioned.

When I introduce people to improv skills, I may start by asking them to play the mirror game. They stand facing their partner, as if each were reflecting the other in a mirror. At first I encourage stillness, though this is nearly impossible. There is always something moving; a breath here, a blink there, a shifting of weight. They must maintain eye contact. That's not easy. Eventually, as the minutes pass, they begin to trust one another to look longer and relax their faces.

Gradually, their movements become attuned, as if they really were in a mirror. Great moments occur when the observer (and even the participants) cannot tell who initiated which gesture because both are doing it, seemingly together. It is the essence of a great improv relationship onstage. We call this Follow the Follower. I take your idea, you take my idea and we share them back and forth, co-creating something over and above our individual contribution.

People and pairs
Some pairings play a competitive game. It may still be collaborative, yet there is a sense of trying to up the ante in terms of the grandness or absurdity of the gesture.

Others play it slow and smooth. Each pair finds its rhythm. It strikes me that it's often about the personality, not of the individual, but of the pair. There is an African word, 'ubuntu', which can't be easily translated but maybe means, 'My humanity is inextricably bound up in yours.' I like the simple phrase, 'I am because of you.'

Where do I look though?
When I was younger, I used to play a game. I would deliberately look at the other person's right eye, then left eye, and see if they noticed. I don't know if they did (sorry, it wasn't very scientific), but in the end it just seemed better to look at both eyes at the same time.

Thankfully Michael Ellsberg agrees and suggests maintaining a general, soft and wide focus. This is a good idea because you don't want to miss out on the information that's coming from the rest of the face.

Ellsberg also says, 'The eyes are the windows to the sale'. Eek.

Doesn't being British mean being wary of the words sale or selling? Sale is only allowed in polite company if preceded by the words 'January' or 'Harrods'.

This is nonsense of course, but it's a lazy stereotype for an easy laugh or a stock character in movies. I did hear a sales rep once say that he didn't want to use the word 'selling' in front of his client because then the client would think that all he cared about was his bonus. Then I reminded him of his own job title: Sales Rep.

Ellsberg quotes a Silicon Valley business coach, Victor Cheng, who says, 'Body language is 80 per cent of sales'. John Petrucci of State Auto Insurance in America, when I told him I was writing a book on people skills said, 'People buy based on emotions and justify the buying decision based on logic. If we can't be meaningful to them on multiple levels, we'll never transact business.' No wonder he's SVP of customer service.

The eyes do much of the talking, not necessarily about what we are thinking but what we are feeling. Paul Ekman is the world's leading expert on facial expression.[2] He talks about micro-expressions: rapid movements of facial muscles that are allied to underlying emotions. Those of us in the theatre know how much an audience picks up on these tiny beats.

I used to keep quiet when these momentary switches happened. I thought perhaps this sort of thing is only of interest to those of us who do professional pretending for a living. I was wrong. Now when I raise the subject, there is ready agreement that these fleeting moments matter.

One of the people who has influenced me most is Frank Farrelly, the father of *Provocative Therapy*, who used humour to help people back to mental health.[3] In many ways it is thanks to him that I dared to bring improv to business. He talked about looking for those tiny moments when someone reacts and the penny drops, when something physical indicates an emotional breakthrough. Often it's the eyes, or the voice, or something in the body. Ultimately it's a shift in energy. You need to be looking or you can easily miss it.

I created a two-day workshop for pharmaceutical sales reps, training them to use improv and story skills in their job, which is to sell to doctors. I called it, 'Whose Script is it Anyway?' (Their shorthand for prescription is 'script'. See what I did there?)

On the second morning we were playing a game called Delight. I was taught it by Keith Johnstone, guru of *Impro* (as his great book is called). In pairs we tell a story and act it out as we go. Only one person speaks, narrating the tale. Both have to act it out together, unless there's something they don't like, in which case they can say 'no'.

Let's say it's Bob telling the story with Barbara. Bob has to rely on Barbara and pick up her vibe from her non-verbal behavior. He has to keep going when she says 'no'. (Have you heard that improv is all about saying, 'yes'? There's rather more to it but we'll explore in more detail later.)

We were playing this in a dull seminar room in one of those mid-market chain hotels somewhere not quite outside London. Bob was not altogether convinced that he had anything to learn, least of all from a ne'er-do-well thespian like me.

His partner Barbara said 'no' clearly and helpfully as they practised. She played along and acted out the story when it worked for her, as per my instruction. The action took them to a bar. The barman approached and Bob suggested a particular cocktail for Barbara, she said 'no'. All of us watching could see that she didn't want a cocktail. She wanted the barman. Well, you know what I mean, she wanted to chat to him.

However, Bob was totally focused on his cocktail agenda. Because he wasn't interested in the barman he just gave her a long list of cocktails on the menu. She said 'no' to all of them. He was offering what he would have wanted, not what his customer desired. His list could not be faulted. It was a great list, for him, a cocktail fan. But he was batting on the wrong pitch.

What had gone wrong? He wasn't looking at her. He may have been looking at his audience momentarily, but mostly he was looking inside himself. Our reaction to her frustration might have made him look at her but all he perceived was, 'No, that's the wrong cocktail', not what she was actually trying to say which was, 'No, that's the wrong subject'.

In the end, she took a cocktail so they could move on but the story never regained the energy of the 'barman moment'. In the debrief afterwards, Barbara admitted what we all knew. Bob was astounded. Only one person in the room had missed her 'customer needs'. Unfortunately, he was the very person who needed to be aware of what she wanted. He had lost the sale. Not only had he not picked up what she wanted, he had compounded the error and annoyed her by going off on a tangent clearly not of her choosing.

The game shows how small things matter. Tiny indications in the eyes or voice or body give so much away – if we are really looking.

Presenting

Here is a useful technical tip for presenting...
Are you ready?

LOOK
AT
YOUR
AUDIENCE

More presenting tips

Do not spend most of your time gazing at your lovely slides. You made them (and if you didn't, you should know them very well by the time you inflict them on an audience) so you have no need to look, other than perhaps a quick glance to ensure that it's the one you expect.

I once spoke at a conference after a politician who just read out his single-spaced type-written-small-font script in front of two hundred people. I looked around the room. Not a single person was engaged. He might as well have handed round photocopies of it and played some light music while we read his wise words to ourselves. Perhaps Vivaldi's The Four Seasons or something by Jean-Michel Jarre?

Give your audience good eye contact. Even if your eyes have to glimpse down at your notes once in a while, your eyes should be on the audience most of the time.

Simple Steps for making speech notes

- Brief bullet points
- Very large font
- Hand-written by you

The effect of writing them yourself means you become familiar with them. Large font means only a quick peek is required now and then.

Your eyes should not be constantly looking at the same person or the same area and you should not be looking above their heads. Spread it around but make sure you do catch individuals' attention for a moment of real connection. Lee Glickstein, founder of Speaking Circles International and quoted in Michael Ellsberg's book, says that we should engage each person we focus on 100% for that moment rather than trying to look at 100% of the people. That intent transfers to everyone else in the audience.

It's tempting to look at the person who seems disengaged. We comedians know that feeling. We spot Mr Non-Laugher. I have often found that the person whose eyes don't seem to be tuning into my meaningful mutterings is the very one who wants to engage afterwards. So don't give up on anyone.

Speeches and leadership

After eighteen years of working with business people I have come to the conclusion that they really ought to become good at public speaking to advance in their career. Leaders need to be seen. It's a career-limiter if you cannot stand in front of your people and explain what you're about.

This can be taught. It can be learned by introverts and extraverts alike, but only if you really want to learn, as I stated in the previous chapter. It is uncomfortable. Standing up and talking in front of other people is not natural. You need to find ways of coping. You need to look right. Looking relaxed and calm involves great rigour. You need to prepare and rehearse your piece as well as breathing or visualisation exercises perhaps. It doesn't just happen by magic.

I hosted a conference for an organisation which had flown six hundred of their leading staff from across the world to a football stadium (not the pitch, but the state of the art conference hall and seminar rooms). They put together a day of interactive events and rich content and even booked Kriss Akabusi to headline. Then on came the CEO. He muttered into a piece of paper some bland words of encouragement he'd scribbled, probably in the tea break prior to his appearance; no eye contact, no commitment. I have seen this so often. The head honcho makes no connection with the staff. It's so simple to make eye contact count and so obvious when it's failed.

Fifty per cent?

Eye contact is as important in real life as in presentations. We have all met people who give eye contact less than 50% of the time and it can be hard to believe they are paying attention to us. The truth is, they actually might be but it just means we have to work through our initial feelings of disconnection.

Why not make it easy for other people? If you are a less-than-fifty-percenter why not increase your eye contact, so others won't doubt your attentiveness? Notice the way you look at people, the way they catch your eyes, and take note of the smallest movements. And try things out.

Send and receive

We send out signals by looking. At the same time, we receive signals by looking.

> The very things that decode what the other person is feeling also betray what we are thinking.

Eyes can say things that might not be allowed in verbal communication. We certainly look for any disconnect between the words and the eyes. And we believe the eyes.

One person I coached worked in the 'back office'. She had to report to the CEO once a month. She said she felt over-awed. Digging a little, I found that she was too scared to look at him. So I suggested we play a game where she pretended that I was him.

She had two colleagues with her. They pretended to be other members of the executive board. I told her to look at all of us equally, including me, the CEO. It was easier than she thought. Her point of concentration was eye contact but guess what? She sat up and her voice became stronger. As I will keep saying in this book, your body and mind do not act in isolation. They are one system.

Luckily there's even a fancy way of describing what we sense to be true. It's called the Embodied Theory of Cognition.[4] Our cognitive processes (conscious and unconscious) are not disconnected from our legs, arms, eyes, ears, sense of touch and so on. You see it in children. They understand the world through touch and smell. They're not just computers that are programmed. They evolve so 'knowing' doesn't just come from 'thinking'. A batsman in cricket doesn't have time to reason where the ball is going but still manages to hit it.

Even the clothes you wear affect your cognitive processes. 'If you wear a white coat that you believe belongs to a doctor, your ability to pay attention increases sharply. But if you wear the same white coat believing it belongs to a painter, you will show no such improvement', found Dr Galinsky of the Kellogg School of Management.

Mirror, mirror; mirror neurons
I did hear that you should dress not for the job you are in, but for the job one up from the one you are in, or the one you want to be in. I'm not sure what your boss would think of that. Perhaps she is dressing for the job she hopes to be in. Maybe it goes all the way to the top? So what does the person at the top of the organisation wear? Perhaps s/he is hoping his/her next job is retiring and should come to work in gardening gear.

I am not an image consultant. But do ask yourself if the impression you create is appropriate to the picture you would like people to have of you. I tend to wear something appropriate to the other person. I don't want to scare the horses. Maybe it's more about the way I feel rather than the external appearance. Those are not two separate things.

I was very excited when I came across mirror neurons.[5] These explain why we feel some of the same sensations that we observe others feeling. In Italy in the early 1990s, researchers were studying macaque monkeys. They put electrodes in their brains to study what happened during different actions including reaching for food. One day they noticed neurons fired in the same area not only when the monkeys were eating but when they were watching one of the researchers pick up his food. They were not doing the action themselves yet something was happening.

A mirror neuron is a special type of brain cell that fires not only when an animal does the action but also when the animal sees someone else do that action. When you see someone else smile, your mirror neurons for smiling gear up, so you experience the feeling associated with smiling.

It's not just the action we are feeling but the intent as well. Different things happen when you see someone pick up a drink compared with when they pick it up to tidy it away. And we decipher facial expressions. Frowning when tasting some yucky food activates the same system as observing someone else doing the same.

We'll discuss smiling in my chapter, Lighten. In the meantime, be aware of the reactions you are setting off in others with your eyes, and they are setting off in you with theirs ...

Simple Steps

- Practise looking at people a little more.

- Enjoy eye contact, don't rush away from it.

- Look for those things which are unspoken but nonetheless important.

- Look at people when you are with them, not at your phone.

STEP THREE
LISTEN

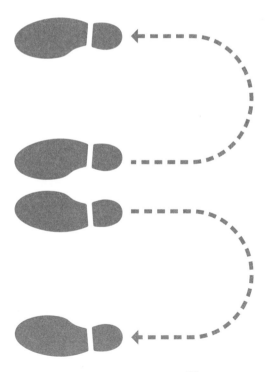

Many of my clients come to me because they want better listening in their organisations:

'We need our sales force to listen to customers'
'Our consultants are not good at listening to the client'
'People aren't really listening to each other'

You may think that improv theatre is about making jokes. No. Improv theatre is an art form which puts listening explicitly at its heart. Listening is the first rule of improv. You are looking with intent for something to build upon. I've even made up my own word based on this. More of that later.

> In improv theatre we listen with intent.

Three listening scenarios

Different situations call for different types of listening. Perhaps you need a response from your boss. Here are three possibilities you might find familiar (with flying metaphors included):

A. 90 seconds: Pop head round the door, just need to sort this now. (Express check-in, boarding pass only).

B. 5 minutes: Shut the office door, need a few moments to check this with you. (Hand luggage in the overhead locker).

C. Can we have coffee or a walk? (Need to check baggage in the hold).

They all require some sort of action. The danger is that you confuse situation A for situation B (or B for C). No point arriving at the gate with excess baggage or heading to the Himalayas with just a toothbrush.

Listen not just for content but for context.

By the way, if you are the initiator of these situations (A, B or C) you should plan them, and make it easy for the other person to know what kind of listening may be needed. Be proactive and think about what they might say or ask. It's amazing how even a brief moment can solve a problem or re-invigorate a stalled project.

> 'When you talk, you repeat what you already know; when you listen, you often learn something.'
> Dalai Lama

What listening is not

The worst kind of listening is just waiting for your turn to speak. As my friend, psychologist Ben Fuchs said, 'sometimes at board meetings, executives are not so much listening as "reloading"'.

Seth S. Horovitz is an Audio Neuroscientist. Wow. He is author of *How Hearing Shapes the Mind*. I found him through his article in the *New York Times* about the difference between hearing and listening.[1] We hear lots of things but for us to listen they need to jump out of the background noise.

Hearing is a sense. Listening is a skill. The difference is attention.

Listening requires attention

Shall I make an equation?

$$Hearing + Attention = Listening$$

Or should it be ...

Hearing x Attention = Listening

Seth thinks that the sense of hearing is underrated, compared with the sense of sight. Apparently thought happens about as fast as visual recognition but we react to a sudden sound ten times faster than that. You might see something out of the corner of your eye and turn to look at it. That could take getting on for a second. Hearing something 'out of the corner of your ear' (my phrase, not his. Sorry Seth!) takes much less time.

Seth calls hearing our 'alarm system'. It's on all the time, wherever our gaze may be and even when we're asleep. However, because there is nowhere really silent, we're used to tuning out most noise unless it signifies danger or something pleasurable.

A sudden loud noise creates a startle. There is a chain reaction from your ears to your spine. In a tenth of a second, five neurons in that chain pass on the message, meaning your heart pumps harder, your shoulders hunch and you look around for the sabre tooth tiger, just like cavemen would have done.

My equation above rather simplifies things. 'There are different types of attention' says Seth, 'and they use different parts of the brain.'

What if you hear your name across a room? There's a more complex pathway but you're still not making meaning. If you are really listening, more of the computing part of the brain becomes involved and less important sounds get tuned out. Yet your alarm system is still on alert for any life-threatening noise.

Hearing is a physical act that we cannot help doing.

Listening is a cognitive skill that requires effort.

And we can improve at it.

Hearing has been around for millions of years and loads of creatures do it without being all that intelligent. However, listening is a skill that requires brain-power.

> 'We think we listen, but very rarely do we listen with real understanding, true empathy. Yet listening, of this very special kind, is one of the most potent forces I know.'
> Carl Rogers

Listening involves:
- Attention
- Respect
- Noticing emotion
- Not jumping to your own conclusions

Active listening

Plenty of management training types talk about active listening. That sounds good, doesn't it? But there seem to be plenty of different interpretations of it. For some it's really, really listening, with lots of nodding and supportive 'uh-huhs'.

One of my favourite experts in this field is Dr Robin Dreeke. He was Head of Behavioral Analysis at the FBI Counter-Intelligence Unit. That's a heck of a job title, isn't it? His book on influence and rapport is called It's *Not All About Me*. He shows how creating rapport begins with listening.

For some it's about putting yourself into the shoes of the person talking. For others, it's about repeating back exactly what is heard. The other day, a very clever barrister (Or was it barista? No he was a QC) admitted he had tried a listening exercise on a mediation course. (Lots of lawyers are qualified mediators now. Perhaps they see the power of a less adversarial approach.) The exercise was simply to repeat back what you heard, word for word.

When it was his turn to be on the receiving end of this active listening, Mr QC said it helped him feel really good, even though he knew exactly what was happening. He felt empowered simply by the other person repeating back.

Remember I said I have invented a new word? It's about listening with intent beyond active listening. My new word is ...

Intentive

(It sounds a bit 'California' doesn't it? Oh well!)

Intentive listening
Have you read a book by Steven Covey called *The Seven Habits of Highly Effective People*? It was all the rage in the nineties and its success and applicability continue. On this subject, he said 'some people listen to respond. You should listen to understand.'

However, this doesn't quite convey the type of listening that the improv performer seeks to achieve. We treat what the other person says as an offer, a gift even, something to be used and added to, in expectation that our response will in turn be treated as an offer to build a story together.

Of course, you don't always know which element of what you have conveyed will be treated as the offer. It might be just one word or concept or an aside or even just your body language.

Be generous

This is why we talk about a generous performer: not generous in terms of giving out stuff, but generous in terms of giving space, taking your offers and making sense of them. A great improv performer gift wraps your offer and lobs it back to you in a way that perhaps you did not imagine yourself. Or maybe exactly as you envisaged. She is there with you and enjoys your problem but could show you a totally different take on it. You may have felt what you said was weak, unfocused, lame and then your generous partner elevates it, enjoys it and becomes your fellow passenger on the journey, as well as your co-pilot.

That's good listening.

It's about understanding your tone, being with you, fumbling together for a way forward, simultaneously pushing while also being pulled to somewhere that feels right because we went there together.

Does this seem too touchy-feely? When you watch a show with an improv troupe like the Comedy Store Players you see all of the above.[2] You may see six performers, sometimes in pairs, sometimes more, guiding each other through moments of ambiguity, flickers of fear, teeing each other up, passing each other the ball, rescuing a situation or finding joy in the ruins, running amok where nothing seemed possible, causing giggles aplenty or just a quiet admiration.

The listening of the improv performer is precise. Mike Myers used to teach us to ask, 'Why, specifically, have the gods of improv given us this scene, at this moment, with these characters?'

From my improv ethos, I go one step further than Stephen Covey. I say:

> Listen such that your response shows you have understood.

What if you don't understand? Well, at least show that you are trying to understand.

> Listen such that your response shows you are understanding.

Hmm, not sure. At my ancient age (84!), I have come to the conclusion that I cannot really understand anyone fully: not even myself. But I want to try to understand at least some bits of the other person, even if just for the moment we are together.

How about:

Maybe that works. But it doesn't mention listening. Oh dear. Although that's the clever thing. Real listening does not draw attention to itself.

Listen, not to judge ...

Robin Dreeke advises us to listen to validate rather than to judge. He talks about listening in a way that echoes the improv ethos, 'Seek out someone else's thoughts and opinions without judging them'. Note that this is NOT the same as agreeing with them. 'Validation is taking the time to understand what their needs, wants, dreams and aspirations are.'

People may be able to tolerate someone disagreeing with them as long as they feel they have been listened to. I find I have made people very angry if I fail to listen to them. Your friends are not necessarily the people who agree with you but the ones who bother to take on board what you have said. They may even find that they are persuaded by your arguments.

Listen slow

Daniel Kahneman, in his book *Thinking Fast and Slow*, shows the dangers of confirmation bias: our tendency only to notice data that backs up our own point of view. This means we are at risk of missing what is going on. We may overlook what is important to the other person because it isn't important to us. That's what *Listening Fast* is.

Perhaps you're just noticing how this situation or person is similar to one you've seen before or how what is being said affects you, rather than putting yourself in the other person's shoes.

I did a module in my sociology course at university called Deviance. It made me look at the assumptions we have which may make us see some people as different, as 'other'. But surely each of us is abnormal in some respect? I know I am.

Listen don't label

Perhaps you have heard of a French philosopher called Michel Foucault. When I read about his Labelling Theory my eyes were opened. Once you hear about one facet of a person, says Foucault, you may find it hard not to see everything about her or him through that single filter. (People also talk about 'Social Amplification of Deviance'.)

It's easy to think all accountants are the same. All English people are the same. All CEOs are the same. (No they are not.)

After running workshops across four continents, with people in all sorts of jobs, I have found this not to be true. It has not surprised me to find that 'we have more in common than things that divide us'.[3] Or is this confirmation bias on my part?

I encourage people to notice the filters through which they listen, to explore their own assumptions and the assumptions people may have about them.

Because I am English and white and speak with an accent known as Received Pronunciation (it used to be called Queen's English but she doesn't talk quite like me) people have very clear assumptions about what sort of person I am. On the other hand, the label 'comedian' carries with it many prejudices.

Not all these assumptions are bad or good but problems arise when we are not aware of them. Think about the assumptions people may have about you based on any or all of the following ...

Gender
Occupation
Height
Education
Accent
Clothing
Religion or lack thereof
Political sympathies or lack thereof
Hobbies
Possible introversion/extraversion

Some of these things you may choose to vary or keep hidden according to the impact you desire. Some you cannot change. But you can change the way you listen to somebody, regardless of the above characteristics.

Listen to learn
Vala Afshar, Chief Digital Evangelist at Salesforce, tweeted his five simple tips for improving listening skills:

1. Speak less
2. Do not interrupt

3. Deep eye contact
4. Focus on message
5. Adopt a beginner's mindset

I think these are great, but ...

Speaking less is a good idea until a canny observation, an incisive question or even an appropriate interruption could actually show real listening. And what is the message? Certainly, some doctors will tell you that the 'presenting issue' which a patient brings initially may not be the one actually concerning them most. That may be the one they mention on their way out... 'Oh and another thing'.

When I was studying coaching at Ashridge Business School, I discovered John Heron's six types of therapeutic intervention that might be undertaken by, say, a doctor or counsellor:

1. Prescriptive
2. Informative
3. Confronting
4. Cathartic
5. Catalytic
6. Supportive

I mention this because it is easy to see listening as just supportive or cathartic 'oh there, there, poor you, let it all hang out, I'll sob with you' ... the ultimate softy of soft skills, perhaps? These six types of listening show there is far more to it than that.

Although sometimes listening is just hearing, being present and saying nothing, but as I said at the beginning of the chapter, there are different types of listening for different types of situations. Don't bring tents and hiking gear for a mini-break in Paris.

Vala Afshar talks about a beginner's mindset. That sounds all nice and Zen but what does it mean on a busy Monday morning? What if you are not a beginner? You know all about the subject and some schmuck is trying to work through something when you know the answer and could just tell them.

I guess I have to go back to my step for Learn. What can you learn from this situation? Maybe your knowing it all is not helping this person? What can you learn about flexing your communication style? Or what can you learn about this person? What can you learn about how they see the world? Perhaps you need a different leadership style for each and every person?

Or you just need to tell them what to do, and save time for everyone. Sometimes, that is what leadership is about, isn't it? But spare at least some time to listen. And judge the situation.

What stops us listening?

I came across a book called *Charisma: Seven Keys to Developing the Magnetism That Leads to Success* by Tony Alessandra. He neatly lines up five reasons why we aren't great at listening:

1. Listening takes effort
2. We screen out stuff
3. We think we already know what the other person is going to say
4. We may never have had training
5. The Listening Gap

What is the Listening Gap?

Apparently, we can listen to many more words per minute than can be spoken per minute. It turns out this is a thing, a proper scientific thing. We talk at about 125 words a minute in normal conversation. (And, please note, my dear presentation students, it should be about 100 words per minute when giving a speech).

We can listen at about 400 words a minute. So there is a gap of about 275 words per minute. What are we doing with that spare mental capacity?

You might think that listening is a passive activity where you just need to keep still. It's not like reading where you can shift, stop, and go back to read a section where you drifted off and found yourself thinking about chocolate chip cookies when you should have been reading about, say, Key Performance Indicators in the Chilled Distribution Supply Chain.

You cannot assume that you have really listened. You cannot assume the other person is fully 'there'. They could be somewhere else. You have to make a conscious effort to block out your own thoughts.

When listening isn't really listening

1. Leaping: jumping too quickly to say, 'Oh yes, I'm just like that' or 'Ooh no, I would never do something like that.'
2. Solutionising: It's easy to want to 'sort it out' too early.
3. Competing: by knowing more about the topic, or humble-bragging 'the same thing happened to me, only much worse...'
4. Detailing: seeing only the trees and not the forest. 'But why were you wearing a hat when you saw the leopard?'

5. Helicoptering: seeing only the forest and not the trees. 'I still think you can be an Olympic swimming champion. Oh? You said you've lost your goggles? Oh who cares where they are.'

Should you recruit for listening?
As automation and algorithms become ever more sophisticated, some technical skills will become redundant but listening will not.

> Wouldn't it be a good idea to hire people
> who are good listeners?

Listening is a conscious, active, cognitive skill that can and should be developed. Listening can help in at least these vital business areas:

Problem-solving
Delegating
Creativity
Finding better ways of working
Using initiative
Working in a team
Being dependable
Seeing a task all the way to completion
Coaching and mentoring others

All these involve listening, don't they? And I'm sure I've missed lots of things out.

Are you a trampoline?
I thought I had nailed a good description of listening: Intentive, seeking not just to hear but to understand. Then I came across a

brilliant *Harvard Business Review* article by Zenger Folkman (a leadership development firm), based on a survey of what great listening really means.[4]

They suggest that most people define good listening as:
- Being quiet if someone is speaking
- Showing you are listening with your face and affirming noises ('mmm ... yes ... really?')
- Being able to paraphrase (or repeat) what you just heard or summarise to check for understanding, 'so what I think you're saying is ...'

That seems right, doesn't it? Yet they went deeper by studying 3,492 people and found 20 things that seemed to set apart those identified as the most effective listeners.

Those 20 factors could be grouped into four main findings:
1. There's much more to great listening than being quiet. It's active, it's a two-way exchange. You might ask questions that promote discovery and insight. You may prod but it's constructive.
2. Good listeners build the other's self-esteem. Being too passive or too critical does not make it positive for the other person. It should feel safe and differences can be discussed openly.
3. It's co-operative not competitive. We know how irritating it is to have someone leaping on our errors of logic or grammar or whatever. It's not about winning, it's about helping, even when that involves disagreement.
4. Giving appropriate suggestions and alternatives is seen as part of listening. This is a skill. It's not about being combative or jumping with ready answers, it's about trust.

Listening is not passive, it is not a spectator sport. Jack Zenger and Joseph Folkman came up with the brilliant metaphor that being a great listener is not like being a sponge, soaking up the information. It's like being a trampoline. You actively find ways to make the other person feel better, about themselves, their feelings and their possibilities. With a trampoline you gain energy, momentum and height.

> You are a great listener if you reflect and bring out more.

We talk a lot about energy in theatre: low energy, wrong energy, even the energy of stillness. I love the idea that listening is about providing energy.

> Are the conversations in your organisations creating or destroying energy?

The 1957

I've read many articles on listening. I thought I had created a cocktail of approaches that is practical and analytical yet sheds light on the topic using the best of 21st century thinking. Then I came across an article that makes many of the same points really well. It is by Ralph G. Nichols and Leonard A. Stevens (I like those spare initials, don't you?) It's from the *Harvard Business Review* ... from 1957, 60 years ago![5]

They surveyed some executives in Chicago. One commented that 80% of his work depended on listening to someone or someone listening to him. Others noted the importance of listening and how things go wrong without it. However, in all the company's considerations about communications, listening was overlooked.

On that subject, I found a recent blog called sklatch.net which has some great writing about listening in conversation. It's written by a chap called Michael Webb. He talks about the supply and demand side of communication. There is plenty of coaching in speaking (supply side) and writing but not much in listening (demand side).

Are these observations about communication still true in today's world of texts, email, WhatsApp, SnapChat, teleconferences, Face-Time and Skype?

Even if that 80% figure is too high for you, what might be a more accurate guess? 60%? Would you agree that it is more than 50% for an enormous number of individuals and organisations?

Nichols and Stevens did some tests which found that two months after listening to a speech, people remembered only 25%. Really? That much? Intriguingly they found that a half to a third is forgotten in the first eight hours. (In my last chapter, Leave, I will explore the two moments that an audience will be most likely to remember.)

In 1957, they estimated that in someone's work life they might have to listen three times as much as they read. Is that true in 2017? Frequently, in my workshops, people bemoan their reliance on email when they could pick up the phone. For international businesses, seeing each other in person (and listening in a way that is impossible via tele- or audio-conferencing) is vital for gaining trust. A friend who coaches such globe-trotting leadership teams insists they get together three times a year.

That sounds expensive, doesn't it? Yet how much do failures in communication cost?

Even 60 years ago, they knew about the difference in listening and speaking capabilities. That Listening Gap means we can be side-tracked, but what if that spare capacity were used to think about what we are hearing – paying attention to the possible inferences, evidence presented (or ignored), summarising main points and especially the non-verbals (face, gestures, vocal tone)?

Nichols and Stevens have a fascinating analogy for listening. It might even beat the trampoline metaphor...

The talker's thoughts can be likened to a church. She unpacks it into small oral packages, which she then sends orally to the listener, who has to reassemble them. But the listener may build up an inaccurate representation.

It's hard enough reconstructing an IKEA wardrobe when you have time and a diagram (and maybe the right Allen key). In conversation, the edifice you build in your mind may be quite unlike the one imagined by the other person. It might be a very different 'church'. Or a barn. Or just a pile of stones and wood.

When I first read this, I did a little jig. Why? Because one of the gurus of improv in the USA in the fifties and sixties, Del Close, said of the improv ethos of collaboration, 'Don't bring a cathedral into a scene. Bring a brick; let us build together'.[6]

This gives us a key to listening. Some people listen for facts. It would be better to listen for ideas, say our friends from 1957. I would go further...

Don't just listen for facts, listen for stories.

One of the most profound exercises I run in my sessions is to ask people in pairs to listen to a story from their partner, then tell that very story back but in the first person, as if it happened to them. It's seemingly about listening and presentation skills, but then really becomes about story, the basic currency of human understanding.

Every time I run this story-swap exercise something profound turns up. It could be about loss, love, family or overcoming the odds. Often something sweet or funny emerges too. We get to know each other via stories more than through CVs, resumes and LinkedIn profiles.

'Listening is the recognition that everyone embodies a biological, emotional & social history.'
R.Strozzi-Heckler

Listening is a vital business skill. I don't care if you call it soft or hard. If you are not listening to your own people at all levels, your customers, your suppliers (for sure), your rivals, other sectors, or to technological news then you will be in trouble.

How many meetings do you attend that are more about talking than listening? It might be interesting for you to make an inventory of a typical day at work. How much of your time is spent listening, compared with other activities? Listening isn't just a fluffy nice-to-have intangible. It's an essential skill and should be a vital part of a company's culture.

The leaders of an organisation should be its best listeners. Actually, I have found this to be so in many instances. They have reached an elevated position because they create the conditions for listening and can interpret well. They can see the church and the bricks. They are looking at other churches and bricks too (have I done too much on that metaphor?)

These days we are told that leadership is not about command and control but more about sense and respond. This makes way for innovation.

Simple Steps

- Look for what else is going on besides the words... body language, emotion, digressions, repetitions, an emerging story.

- It's okay to anticipate to keep your attention. Were you right? That can help you to understand. Were you wrong? Why? Notice the difference.

- Summarise what's being said... in your head and out loud.

- Listen to learn and imagine what you could build.

STEP FOUR
LINK

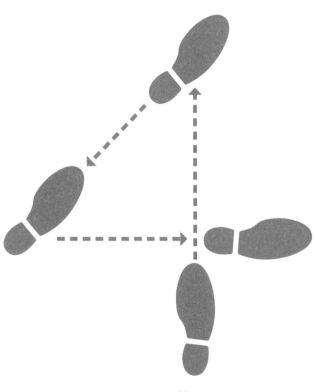

I did think hard about combining Step Three, Listen, with this Step, which I have called Link. Much of what I say should not be taken separately. The Seven Ls are not distinct, discrete ploys. They are just different, overlapping aspects of getting on better with people.

Listen/Link could be considered almost the same action. What do I mean by that? It's my Intentive thing …

> You show that you have listened by how you link what you say (or do) to what you have heard.

Yes, And

In improv we have a warm-up/training drill called Yes, And. You start each utterance with those words. Some workshop partici-pants say to me that this isn't the way people talk in real life. Perhaps not. It's too difficult, they say.

I find it interesting that even in a game, some people find it hard to say yes. The stakes are low. They are playing characters, not themselves. Yet saying yes seems hard. In the fifties and sixties, the originators of improv found that 'yes' worked better than 'no' through trial and error. Accepting the offer improved the story.

It might be easy to find reasons to say no. What is fun and creative is to find interesting ways to say yes to someone. That's where the 'And' of 'Yes, And' comes in. We even use 'YesAnd' as a verb or noun in its own right. 'Here's a YesAnd'. They are not separate.

We accept the offer: Yes

Then we give an offer based on the offer that we are given: And

This is why I feel Listen-Link could be one notion. The link you convey to what you have heard shows that you have listened. But there is more to it. Of course, in real improv scenes in the theatre, as in real life, we don't need to say the actual words 'Yes And'. We have other ways of listening and linking.

Imagine an improv scene of two people in a restaurant:
A: This soup is delicious.
B: Yes, and it's the chef's specialty.

B has accepted the offer of soup then added something, thus validating the soup offer.

How about this?
A: This soup is delicious.
B: No, it's not.

Here, B has rejected the offer of 'delicious', you could say, but accepted the offer of 'soup'. You can see why Yes, And can be misunderstood. I have met people who have been taught it badly. I have met people who admit that they have taught it badly. Apparently it was featured on the satirical comedy show, *The Thick Of It*, where it went horribly wrong because the participants did not understand the ethos.

A journalist attended one of my workshops and wrote about it for the *Financial Times*. She wrote about the 'And, Yes' exercise. Oh dear. Saying ' And, Yes' is meaningless. Every once in a while, somebody in my workshops also thinks the exercise is, 'And, Yes' even after I have explained it, then demonstrated it with a participant. I would love to know why (other than my poor explanation): Is 'Yes, And' so alien to some people?

So I will try to make this clear now.

'Yes' is accepting the offer. It's intriguing how some people rebel and don't want to say yes, even when it's an exercise to help them learn. Perhaps they want to control the conversation.

Accepting the other person's offer is not the same as simply acquiescing. I always try to explain that Yes, And is an exercise to strengthen your improv muscle (your Listen-Link neural pathway) Accepting someone's offer in real life may hardly ever involve using the actual word 'yes'.

At one of the world's leading management consultancy firms, one chap came up to me and said, 'Oh you're the YesAnd guy! I know this technique. You say "yes, and" when you really mean "yes, but"'.

He clearly thought that Yes, And was some sort of hypnotic trick. Just by saying 'yes, and' you could fool the other party that you weren't dissing their idea.
'Yes, and we can't afford that'
'Yes, and the executive team won't like that'
'Yes, and I don't like you'

NO!

Tina Fey has a brilliant summary of the improv ethos in her book, *Bossy Pants*. She simply says that accepting the other person's offer (Yes) is to respect what he or she has created. The And is about contributing something of your own. 'It's your responsibility to contribute', she says.

Take a look at this:
A: I like your tie.
B: I'm not wearing a tie.

This is something we call a Block. B explicitly turned down the offer of tie. You could say that listening has taken place because B has used the word tie but he has denied the reality of said tie. However, it could still be an offer in disguise. It depends what A does with it. It's what we do together. (It's 'relational' if you really want the organisational development/business school jargon).

Here is a similar example:
A: This soup is delicious.
B: No it's not.

What could happen next that is an offer and not a block?
A: This soup is delicious.
B: No it's not. Usually it is. Maybe there's a new soup chef.

See what I did there? And this is an opening for A:
A: Yes there is. He's my boyfriend.

See how playing the game is creative? But note that in the YesAnd dynamic, A or B can choose what they specifically decide to build the And on.

Without getting too self-indulgent, can I point out that A makes B right? Because of what A did, the scene continues and only in hindsight (when we have a great scene about the soup-chef boyfriend) can we say what a brilliant offer the words 'no, it's not' turned out to be.

What people may say is one thing. What we do with it is what matters. That's why linking is such an essential skill.

You might say this is all well and good in your silly, make-believe sketches and made-up-on-the-hoof game but I'm running a business where you can't just pull things out of the air.

I want to make it clear that Yes, And is an ethos which can inspire and motivate. It is adaptable for meetings, coaching, negotiations, leadership and beyond.

It is creative. It allows for ambiguity and diversity and beckons innovation. You may rarely use the words 'yes' or 'and' together but you can still be YesAnding.

What if my job is to say, 'yes, but'?
Now here's a little insight which I have found when working with 'non-fee-earners' (I hate that phrase). I'm talking about compliance, legal, procurement, logistics, IT, finance, the type you think would be all about blocking, saying no or YesButing. Actually, I have found they would much rather be YesAnding. So they need to be invited in early when an idea or project is brewing. I like to encourage them to find ways of being in the midst of things.

Rather than ask them at the last minute, 'Can we do this?' or 'What are the legal ramifications of this?', ask them upfront: 'what could we do?' They would much rather be telling you what you can do at the outset rather than what you cannot do later on down the line when you're all excited about doing that deal which is on shaky ground.

Zen and the art of soup

Let's look at another response to my soup dialogue offer.

A: This soup is delicious.

B: There is no soup. There's nothing there. I don't know what you're talking about.

That's really 'block-y' isn't it? Yet the great improviser still has the chance to come back with:

A: Yes, you're right. I keep imagining soup. I can't help it. Yesterday I was at the dentist and I asked him to take the croutons away.

The improv performer, A, has taken B's seeming negation as an offer of 'I keep imagining soup'. You can see why Robert Poynton has written a book about improv called, *Everything's An Offer.*[1] I mentioned this once to Lee Simpson (one of my brilliant colleagues in the Comedy Store Players and a superb director) and he said, 'You could just as well write a book called, *Everything's a Block*'.

So it's how we frame things which makes the difference. I know very little about martial arts but I understand you need to use the energy of the other person. In tennis, we use the power of the serve in our return.

Work with what the other person gives you, not against it.

So that is the improv approach. We know it works onstage because thousands of shows every night across the globe prove it. But how else could we apply the concept of Link to your business?

Creative connections

Paul Plsek (of DirectedCreativity.com) defines creativity as bringing together two hitherto unconnected ideas.[2] It's the link that counts, not necessarily thinking up a new idea.

The previous soup examples have shown how an obstacle can actually act as a catalyst for a creative breakthrough. There are plenty of scientific, business and military examples of this, where a block became an offer.

Simon Woodroffe, who created Yo! Sushi, lost the lease on his Soho premises for a year; he recognises that some of his best ideas came during that 12-month delay. Post-it Notes came from a failed glue that didn't stick too well. And penicillin ... isn't that because someone forgot to tidy up the lab?

Common ground

It is helpful to find commonality with the other person. I have seen networking advice 'for people who hate networking' which is about finding something you share... experience, education, hobbies.

Dale Carnegie of *How to Win Friends and Influence People* advised us to 'talk in terms of the other person's interests'. Robert Cialdini,

King of Influence, encourages us to find things we have in common quickly, to create trust. It really doesn't have to be profound. You can take a look at their online activity if you are meeting them in advance. You can't do that when meeting someone spontaneously but make it an early target to find some common ground.

I suppose one view of evolutionary psychology is that our ancestors were likely to share their food with those who seemed to have something in common with them. Perhaps we are still thinking that. Certainly we seem to place an importance on reciprocation.

Robin Dreeke talks about listening to validate. Start from the other person's point of view and try to build a link to your own, rather than slamming yours down on the table. Saying, 'I hadn't thought of it like that' is very different from saying, 'That is a bad idea'.

However, Herminia Ibarra warns us to be aware that we are naturally narcissistic and lazy. We look to spend time with, or hire people, like ourselves. Proximity comes a close second to similarity in terms of who we are influenced by, says her research. We don't want to be bothered looking too far for advice. Establishing common ground creates initial rapport with someone new. Just be wary if your network settles into simply being people who think like you or that you see every day.

Duff links

Beware of the bad link. I coached a marketer from a global energy company. She was working alongside a colleague and things were fine. Then suddenly they were not. For three weeks he cold-shouldered her. Perhaps he was not even aware of the change.

She was bold enough to ask him why. He did her the courtesy of telling her. It was all down to one word she used. Just one word!

Okay, it was quite a big word. Not just 'cheese'. It was the name of an agency that she had collaborated with. He had also worked with them but it had ended badly. He didn't even know if they had interacted with the same people. Just the name of the company put him off her. Luckily, she was able to turn things around after this moment but it shows that our joint pasts could have good and bad sides.

Speaker-listener neural coupling

I always used to think that it was a mistake to anticipate what someone was saying, in case you miss something. However, in the previous chapter I suggested that it could be good use of your spare capacity, thanks to the Listening Gap.

Then I found a brilliant piece of research by Greg J Stephens, Lauren Silbert and U Hasson.[3] The production of speech and its comprehension are normally studied as separate processes, but Greg and his posse looked at them together and found that 'the speaker's activity is spatially and temporally coupled with the listener's activity.' (Are you thinking what I'm thinking? Mirror neurons?)

When things are going well the listener's brain activity mirrors that of the speaker, but with a slight delay. When they are going really well, the listener's brain exhibits predictive anticipatory responses.

To use the brick analogy from the previous chapter, as you package small pieces of the church (i.e. you're trying to explain your idea), I am putting them together using similar brain activity and maybe I start building my version before you lob your bricks over to me in your speech.

> So you are preparing to link when you listen well.

When you are actively engaged you are not just hearing sounds. You are using lots of your brain and this can induce a shared contextual model of the situation. Groovy!

That's why I say listen for story. You are not just drawing a plan of the church but building it together. Extra-linguistic areas of the brain are discerning beliefs, desires and goals of others. This coupling of production and comprehension ties in with what lots of people have said for years (actors, philosophers, psychologists), that perception and action are not easy to differentiate.

> Thinking and doing are not separate.

As Elliot Aronson, distinguished psychologist, and author of *The Social Animal* says, 'If you want a more powerful change to take place, you will try to evoke a change in behaviour first; attitudes will follow.'[4]

Link your verbal and non-verbal
Noah Goldstein, co-author with Robert Cialdini and Steve J. Martin of *Yes! 60 Scientifically Proven Ways to Be Persuasive*, says you should link your body language depending on how you would like to influence someone.

If you want to show how attractive your proposition is, be animated, lean forward, move and speak quickly. If you want to increase the attractiveness of an offer, think upbeat and sell-y.

On the other hand, if you want to reduce resistance to your suggestion, it's quite different. Try speaking slower. Be particular with your gestures. Reduce your movements.

Another good ploy is to mimic the body language of the other person. Goldstein cites research that 78.8% bought a product from mimickers, compared with 61.8% from non-mimickers. Customers might not know you are mimicking. After the sale, the customers of mimickers tended to be more upbeat both about the shop and the people who served them.

Perhaps this isn't your style. But be aware that you shouldn't let your body language be too far from the other party and certainly not in direct opposition to your verbal language. That can have a negative impact. You lose trust.

Simple Steps for selling

- Be energetic to sell

- Slow down to reduce resistance

- Copy the customer's energy

If you have encountered Neuro-Linguistic Programming or NLP (don't worry if you haven't), you might know the concept of Matching. There are good reasons to believe that we can create rapport by linking our body language to the other person's... their handshake, the type of words they use, their way of sitting, their energy and even the rhythm of their breathing. First you establish rapport, and only then can you seek to influence the other person. They call it Match, Pace and Lead. It works for plenty of people.

Remember, whatever you do, you should be thinking about the impact that you are having. I suspect that in business we might be looking and listening to see how this person or situation is similar to one we have experienced before. Remember Foucault and 'thinking fast'? Yes, it's good to be looking for things we may share in common with others but dangerous if you are just looking for signs that mean you can put them in a neat pre-existing box.

> 'At the core of earning someone's trust is convincing them that you are dealing with them as a human being, and not as a member of a group or class or subset.'
> David H. Maister et al.[5]

Networking, not twerking?

Does the word 'networking' make you feel a little, um, sordid?

I read somewhere that if you hate this sort of thing, don't think of yourself as a participant but as a host. You are there to make it less ghastly for everyone else. That is a brilliant re-framing of the situation.

Think about it as a linking exercise. You are linking people to each other. So it is really helpful to think of common interests other people have. If you focus on learning, and think about what you can give, rather than take, you will find the whole thing less fraught.

How to make a good introduction

In her book, *The Art of Conversation: A Guided Tour of a Neglected Pleasure*, Catherine Blythe suggests saying two things about a person, not just who they are but why they would be of interest to the other person.[6] It needn't be a job title but how they link to the moment you are in... the location, the event, what you are eating/ drinking/wearing/feeling. Explicitly find things in common, big or small, grand or granular.

> Keep looking for ways to link other people into the conversation.

> Simple Steps for networking

- Get in early

- Link up with that person who looks alone

- Ask to be introduced to someone

- Use people's stories to link them with others

First impressions

Robin Dreeke, the FBI dude, has lots of advice on creating links on first meeting someone. One of his very useful practical exercises is the Third Party Reference. With non-threatening body language and vocal tone you ask a stranger's advice about something they are carrying. 'Is that a good book?' or 'Ooh I like fish fingers too'. So the link is not you to me but you/me to something or someone else. It's effective.

We British tend to choose the weather. Try noticing something else as an opener.

Then there is Dreeke's Sympathy or Assistance Theme. People react well to this, 'I was hoping you could help me...'

> Asking for advice is a great way to make a link.

But not too big a request. Asking, 'Do you know which aisle the frozen peas are on?' may work better than, 'How can I sort out my mess of a life?' (Of course, it's just possible that frozen peas could be the answer to the latter.)

Keep on linkin'

At work, you may be trying to move a project forward. Don't wait for that big meeting to link up with others. Find allies beforehand. Explain your idea. Re-work it in the light of what others say. Practise making links every day; even on the way to the toilet or canteen. Try a smile or a hello or 'I thought of you the other day' as you pick up an earlier topic of conversation. Even better if it was one that made both of you laugh.

Send people quick emails with something that's of value to them once in a while... an article, some information or name of someone who could help them with an issue you know they are dealing with.

Small talk, big talk?

Some people tell me that they can't do small talk...
'I can't think of what to say'
'It feels shallow'
'Where do I start?'

Nicholas Epley, a psychologist at the University of Chicago, looked into this with his student Juliana Schroeder. They experimented with passengers and drivers on trains and buses and even in cabs.

There appeared to be a general assumption that people didn't think others would want to talk to them. This turned out not to be true. There's a great name for this: Pluralistic Ignorance. Many people think one thing and then incorrectly assume that others disagree. Or more often (as I have observed in organisations), a majority of group members reject a norm but go along with it grudgingly just because they think everyone else has bought into it.

There is an understandable fear of feeling trapped if someone opens a conversation with you. This is why Robin Dreeke's 'artificial time constraint' is such a brilliant idea. No stranger wants to commit to a long conversation but if you mention that you have only five minutes, or you are heading out or you are late for something, people will be much more likely to engage because they know it will be brief. It's clearly a 'quick link' moment, so the stakes are low. Of course, Dr Dreeke often finds when he tries this that such low-stake connections can grow later when time is unconstrained ...

Plenty of people enjoy chatting with others more then they expect (Nicholas and Juliana found this across all personality types). Will Fleeson, Psychology Professor at Wake Forest University, found that introverts were actually happier when acting as extraverts. Remember 'act your way into a new way of thinking'?

The problem is how to start it. How to make that opening link? Epley describes it as 'a speed bump at the top of a hill'. Once you are over that tricky first moment, things will flow.

Anthropologist Bronislaw Malinowski wrote about small talk in his 1923 essay, *The Problem of Meaning in Primitive Languages* (wouldn't it be great if someone updated this essay, and included the 'primitive' language of text-speak? Look at texts and WhatsApp and you find very little of value. Or so it might appear.)

Malinowski differentiated between communicating ideas and establishing personal bonds. (The latter he called phatic communion. I was very pleased to discover that phatos in Greek means spoken. This made me think of the nineties dance duo Phats & Small. Perhaps they were Greek scholars, originally called Phatos & Small Talk? Or not.)

Malinowski wrote that small talk was to fill silence, which some people find threatening. (Of course, you should not feel threatened by silence! See my next chapter called Let). He looked down on 'relationship chat' versus 'task-oriented' or 'informational' talk. Is this a man thing?

Justine Coupland has written a book called *Small Talk* with a feminist critique of views that calibrate some forms of communication as superior to others. She teases such a western perspective that 'real talk is talk that "gets stuff done", where "stuff" does not include "relational stuff"'.

What about that famous quote, 'Culture eats strategy for breakfast', often attributed to management guru, Peter Drucker? I guess the point is that lovely strategy documents won't breed success if you have an unengaged workforce. But shouldn't culture and strategy be twinned? Rather than one eating the other for breakfast, shouldn't they be having a light lunch together, gossiping, laughing but also seeing about how they can work together before the bill comes?

However, relational stuff does matter. The reason many people leave their job is because of their manager. The social chat in organisations is highly potent. People talk about the 'mood music', the 'mutterings' and the 'bongo drums'. They reference the importance of what is not in the official press release or the mission statement on the website but what people are actually talking about and feeling.

Speech operates on two levels: semantic (what the words mean) and social. The latter is inseparable from context (tone, body language, environment, previous encounters).

Just notice over the course of a day how much of your communication is social. Of course, the two are not always separate but it's worth being aware of the two dynamics. Small talk shows we have things in common, we belong, and finds areas for agreement (and thus lack of threat).

I am sure you can think of someone who is a great public speaker but isn't so comfortable with people one-on-one. And vice-versa. But I hope this book shows that you can learn to be better at both. There are habits to evolve and 'muscles' to train.

It's very important, however, that the distinction between social and semantic is held lightly. It would be a caricature if you imagine that a 'good' business conversation would go like this:

A: Hello. I like your shoes.

B. Thank you. Your shoes are excellent. Isn't the weather interesting?

A: Yes it is. I have an umbrella like yours.

B: Great. I bought it when I was at a cricket match.

A: Really? I see the England batsmen failed again in India yesterday.

B: Yes, I was up early this morning to watch it.

A: But you don't look in the least bit tired.

B: Thank you.

(Pause)

A: I see you have our office furniture brochure.

B: Yes, and you are such an agreeable fellow that I will buy everything immediately at the price you quote.

I am really trying to encourage you to look for links with the other person, whether they be social or semantic or both. I have heard of healthy relationships forged entirely through the 'real stuff' of business, not the social chit-chat over biscuits or on the golf course.

One leader told how he had this really penny-pinching, tough-minded supplier. It got to the negotiation. They went head-to-head. Each respected the other but drove hard for their end of the bargain. Yet they did come to an agreement and are now good friends, precisely because of that heated moment.

Simple Steps

- 'Think Link' as your first priority.

- Link what you say to what matters to the other person.

- Summarise what the other person says.

- Link your actions to your promises and to your body language.

STEP FIVE
LET

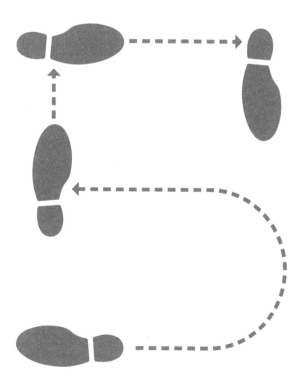

Originally Let was about letting others speak, not correcting them, giving space and time (and tolerance of an opposing view). Then it became about letting yourself have a pause as well or letting yourself off the hook if you make a mistake.

Let there be pauses.

It's easier to listen if you let the words hang in the air for a beat. Think of that as both speaker and listener. I hammer this home when teaching presentation skills. Your audience needs a beat to 'hear' what you just said, to consider it.

It's just as important when you listen in conversation. There is no need to jump in with a response. Wait a beat and you might allow the other person to say something more valuable. In that seemingly awkward moment they may come up with something really important they might not otherwise have shared.

> 'The right word may be effective, but no word was ever as effective as a rightly timed pause.'
> Mark Twain

This is so true, in conversation and certainly in presentations. Slow your pace. Slowing down means you will appear more relaxed (because you are) and you will seem more trustworthy.

As with all these things there are caveats. You might choose to go quicker to raise the urgency of the issue. Varying pace in presentations can add drama and help the audience stay engaged. You might want their hearts to start pumping as you warn them of something bad, then slow down as you offer the prospect of a solution. (Remember Noah Goldstein and linking verbal and non-verbals?)

Think of Barack Obama. Slow and measured, 'Yes we can'. (For lots more insight into oratory and speech-making, read Simon Lancaster's book, *Winning Minds*).

Let the other person speak.

Paul Z. Jackson, author and facilitator, writes about 'short turn taking' in his book *Life-Pass*. It means you are paying attention to the other person, and that sometimes you lead, sometimes you follow. You 'riff' together.

Self-disclosure

If you let people talk they will warm to you. Let them talk about themselves. We love to talk about ourselves, don't we? We all know this but Adrian F. Ward, when writing in the *Scientific American* on The Neuroscience of Everybody's Favourite Topic, says that talking about ourselves feels good. There are biochemical reasons for this.

The Harvard University Social Cognitive and Affective Neuroscience Lab (great name for a band!) even looked at the activity in various neural regions when we talk about ourselves. The areas that lit up are generally associated with reward and have been linked to the pleasurable feelings associated with sex, cocaine and a good meal. Really?

(They don't seem to have quantified this. Where does talking about yourself rank in the league table? Maybe they had to get some poor bloke to talk about himself then go and have a good meal, then have cocaine and then sex. I hope he had chance for a lie down and a cup of tea in between.)

When he worked in the FBI, Robin Dreeke says that many of his 'human sources' liked their FBI handlers more than many of their friends, family or colleagues. Perhaps that's because the encounter was all about them talking rather than the FBI person, unlike their everyday conversations. The FBI person gave lots of attention and wasn't going to drift off or take a phone call.

We spend 60% of the time talking about ourselves, according to a 1997 paper by Robin Dunbar and chums.[1] (How does this work by the way? If you and I are chatting, and you are talking about yourself 60% of the time, and I'm talking about myself 60 % of the time, that adds up to 120%. Maybe we talk on top of each other? Or do I still carry on talking about myself when you've nipped out to the loo?)

On social media the proportion we talk about ourselves is apparently 80%. Yes, that seems about right, doesn't it?

Self-disclosure feels great, even when there is nobody listening, they found. Though it does feel better if the other party is still there. And it's mutual. As we disclose information about ourselves, we like each other more. These social bonds help physical survival, happiness, teamwork and personal growth. So perhaps we've evolved that way. Does it feel good because it leads to other adaptive advantages?

Let other people know about yourself
Self-disclosure can be a helpful leadership trait. It helps gain trust.

When I was an actor in plays, we told each other more about ourselves from day one of rehearsals and more quickly than 'normal people' might do when starting a job. We knew we'd have to work together in tough circumstances so we fast-tracked. In conventional settings, people have months to navigate intimacy. Showbiz folk might have only weeks, or sometimes hours if it's a film or TV shoot.

This is called 'swift trust' in a *Harvard Business Review* article from June 2013, entitled Building Trust Through Skillful Self-Disclosure (why they have two Ls, I don't know. Even American spell-check raises a virtual eyebrow).

Self-disclosing leaders can generate trust and teamwork. If you let people know your thinking or the model you are using, you will enhance performance. You can share examples of your tough experiences or knock-backs, but there is a line not to be crossed (maybe that's why it's 'skillful' with a double L). If in doubt, ask someone first, before breaking down in tears in the office canteen as you reveal your father laughed at you for not being good at football.

Let people have their opinions

Do not correct the other person, let them elaborate and acknowledge that they are making valid points. Let the other person be right. As Dale Carnegie said, 'Show respect for the other person's opinions. Never say, "You're wrong"'.

When someone corrects you on something, you feel a disconnect. You immediately start looking for a chance to do a revenge-correct on the other person. You might rake up an ancient misdemeanour, apparently to make yourself feel better at the other person's expense.

'And another thing – you were wrong last Christmas about the capital of Mongolia! It's Ulan Bator, actually!'

'But Jeffrey, we're talking about why you forgot to buy milk today.'

Try the opposite approach. 'Praise every improvement', said Dale Carnegie. My friends from The Solutions Focus approach suggest Positive Gossip. Instead of muttering behind people's backs about their shortcomings, try talking about their good moments in front of them. You'll find there will be more of them to note in the future. It's a virtuous circle.

Let it go, let it go

Recently I observed two people who were pleased to find they had something in common, they both knew a town particularly well. Then one said something about the town, which the other said was not true. Then he proceeded to try and pull rank by mentioning his job, which meant he should know that piece of information. Neither gave way.

There are times when we just need to let things pass. Robin Dreeke talks about suspending your ego. We have a selfish survival instinct so this may be difficult if someone has just said something mistaken. But it could be useful to pause just for a moment before leaping in and ask ...

Where will this get me?

How much does it matter? As soon as you point out someone else is wrong, he or she feels their self-esteem is under attack. Don't waste that on something trivial. It's hard to admit you are wrong, isn't it? Our brain fights against it.

Cordelia Fine wrote a book called *A Mind of Its Own*, subtitled *How Your Brain Distorts and Deceives*. In moments of stress (which includes fear and distrust), cortisol floods the brain. Higher functions like compassion or building of trust shut down and you can forget anything as tricky as thinking strategically.

Shame comes from being caught in the wrong. Then neurochemistry takes over. Your body cannot regulate emotions or cope with the gap between reality and perception. You might have heard of 'Fight or Flight' but there is another element. Imagine you're in a meeting at work and there's a disagreement, with raised voices talking over each other and you want to convince everyone that you are right. Here are those three options:

Fight – keep going with the argument

Flight – hide behind the group consensus

Freeze – shut up and disengage

All of these may lead to a less than productive conversation, but the fight response is hardest to come back from. When you argue and win, those feel-good hormones, adrenaline and dopamine, surge through your brain. Who wouldn't want to experience that every time?

You (or your boss) may often be right but you could be addicted to the high of winning, not noticing the effect it has on others; they might go to flight, freeze or fight and the possibilities for collaboration could be reduced.

Judith E. Glaser, in a 2013 article for the *Harvard Business Review*, suggests ways we can overcome our 'addiction to being right' with some rules for meetings.

Simple Steps for meetings

- Set rules of engagement: list who is going to speak, so everyone has a chance, not just the loudest voice.

- Give more time for people to explain their ideas without being interrupted.

- Listen more, speak less.

By the way, Susan Cain suggests that introverts write and rehearse what they are going to say and say it early. That helps you set the tone of the meeting. Otherwise the tone could be set by someone else (who may just have the loudest voice).

Arguing

What about when it really matters? When you have decided it IS worth arguing? You are right and the other person is clearly wrong and there will be negative repercussions if the mistaken view persists.

We've all been there, haven't we? Somebody you know well (or not) is holding out for some absurd notion that you just cannot let pass. The tendency is to raise your voice or to repeat your point or simply sulk.

The philosopher Daniel Dennett in his book, *Intuition Pumps and Other Tools for Thinking*, has four rather good rules for arguing intelligently. They are all about making links with your opponent and what they say. It's too easy to ignore or caricature your opponent's position. Dennett himself adapted the rules from Anatol Rapoport, a mathematical psychologist associated with game theory and systems theory:

1. Summarise your opponent's point of view fairly so that they are left thinking, 'Hey you said it even better than I could have done'.

2. Make it clear your areas of agreement, the more specific the better.

3. List what you have actually learned from the other party.

4. OK, now you can rebut their shtick!

Dale Carnegie, in his seminal book *How to Wine Fiends and Influenza People* (is that the title?) says simply, 'The only way to get the best of an argument is to avoid it'. I know some people feel better for a really good argument (and we've seen there may be chemical reasons for that), but we know what Mr Carnegie means, don't we? He says, 'Let the other person save face.'

It's all about saving face but 'if you are wrong admit it quickly and emphatically'. That is much better than carrying on and regretting it later. (Note: please could someone remind me of this advice here at frequent intervals, say once a day?)

Let yourself make mistakes

It may turn out that you put everything into practice that I humbly offer in this book. Your life becomes perfect.

Or not. Maybe you will make a mistake. You say the wrong thing. You just get off on the wrong foot with someone. Or you say something to someone you know well which was ill-judged, hurtful or counterproductive. Is that the end of your life?

No. There are things you can do. Research shows that a complaining customer whose complaint is dealt with well can become more loyal. So don't give up on anyone. Your first mis-step need not be terminal.

Can you be both humble and confident?

Tony Tjan, author and entrepreneur, says that respect requires a balance of humility and confidence: 'You need enough self-confidence to command the respect of others, but that needs to be counter-balanced with knowing that there is much you simply don't know'. Humility is the path towards earning respect, while self-confidence is the path towards commanding it.

Let there be silence

As well as allowing pauses when others are speaking, and when we are speaking, think about having some really long pauses. I mean some actual moments of sustained silence. It is really good for you according to Daniel A. Gross who wrote about silence for Nautilus.com.[2]

Often we have to work hard to achieve silence. People and things around us create noise. In 2011 the World Health Organisation concluded that 340 million people in Western Europe annually lost a million years of healthy life because of noise, and that three thousand heart disease deaths were the result of excessive noise.

In a 2006 study of music, Dr Luciano Bernardi (cardiologist and associate professor at the Department of Internal Medicine, University of Pavia, Italy) found, by chance, that silence was actually more relaxing than 'relaxing' music. Then Imke Kirste (Duke University Medical Centre) discovered, again by accident, that silence had a profound effect on the brains of mice. Two hours of silence in a day brought about the development of cells in the hippo-campus. But Robert Zatorre (expert on the neurology of sound at McGill University in Canada) contends that there is no such thing as silence because 'in the absence of sound, the brain often tends to produce internal representations of sound.'

It seems that the brain is never doing nothing. When we start doing something that needs concentration, its energy consumption only increases a few per cent. At rest the brain has not clocked off. It is dealing with information, trying to make sense of how the internal and external worlds correlate. In an evolutionary sense, not much energy or effort is required to detect a predator since the engine is still ticking over and we don't have to wait for the key to be put into the ignition.

A period of silence every day is good for your mental and physical health. People talk a lot about mindfulness. I think many business meetings would be better if people just sat in silence together for a couple of minutes before they even started. It would bring a focus and a sense of community that verbal exchanges can't always muster.

Dallas Caley, a senior software developer, wrote a piece for Quora.com explaining why programmers need long periods of silence when working. You need to hold a series of steps in your head (like playing chess where you must consider a sequence of moves without touching any pieces). He says that it takes him 15 to 30 minutes to get back on track if he is interrupted.

John Cleese, in a famous 1991 lecture on creativity (do watch it on YouTube), said that you need to give yourself an hour and a half because it takes thirty minutes to get in the zone, you can't just pick up where you left off. He differentiates between the Open Mode (coming up with ideas) and the Closed Mode (implementing those ideas). You need to know which one you are in, and be able to switch when necessary. You can't be creative in the Closed Mode and yet that is where we spend so much of our time at work.

I encourage my coaching clients to put in their diaries something that looks important, 'Project Zeus!', or something which is actually nothing. But it's a specific time (and hopefully space) sealed off from the day-to-day. It should be a time for reflection, maybe a walk. Only they or their PAs know what it really is and it must remain sacrosanct. Seek out opportunities for silence.

Simple Steps

- Let there be pauses.

- Let the other person have their moment.

- Let yourself have an off day... and a day off.

- Let yourself out early from that networking event if you're not in the right frame of mind.

- Let people know you appreciate their work.

- Let people get on with their job.

- Seek out silence.

STEP SIX
LIGHTEN

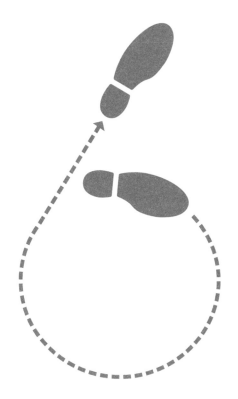

There are two aspects of Lighten I will address. Firstly, humour. You won't be surprised a comedian thinks laughing is important. There is plenty of it in my workshops but as I work with corporate groups it's clear that there is not much laughter in their day-to-day interactions. If nothing else, I feel I have done my job if I give them the chance to laugh together just for a day.

Secondly, I would also like you to think about lightening your body. Caroline Goyder, in her great book *Gravitas*, is keen that we don't see gravitas as heavy (grave, gravity) but as balance. Posture is important for your general health but also for how you are perceived, not just by others but by yourself.

Humour is a leadership tool

Humour allows, encourages, and is a sign of a creative environment. Humour shows you are human. I am not thinking of gags, jokes or stupid pranks. A leader who can laugh at him or herself will be a better leader. When times are tough, humour can make things feel not so bad. Laughing at your past mistakes helps your team think that they too can survive after a setback. Most profoundly, humour shows us perspective. Every situation can be looked at from another point of view.

> 'There is little success where there is little laughter.'
> Andrew Carnegie (no relation)

I cannot think of any reason why appropriate humour should not be part of everybody's daily life and work. This is easy, often spontaneous, humour where the 'butt' of the joke is merely our shared human fallibility.

'Jokes' that mock and divide are not humour. They are the weapons of the bully. The way the word 'banter' (or 'bants', aaargh!) is misused shows exactly this. Laughing to create a disconnect or rupture between people is not humour. It's aggression. I can personally attest that there is a danger of being hurtful even if you think your intent is benign.

Humour encourages creativity, resilience and engagement.

What if you're not that funny? Fine. Just allow some humour to emerge gently. Don't go out and buy a joke-book. If people are not laughing IN your department, they may well be laughing AT it elsewhere.

> 'A sense of humour is part of the art of leadership, of getting along with people, of getting things done.'
> Dwight D. Eisenhower

Ideas are fragile and vulnerable and need a playful, not judgmental, environment to emerge. Peter Sims, in his book *Little Bets*, shows how small discoveries can lead to breakthrough ideas. Many of the best ideas have started like this. They need nurturing and humour certainly helps that.

In 2012 the Bell Leadership Institute conducted a study involving 2,700 people over different environments.[1] People were asked about strengths of senior colleagues. Sense of humour was ranked highest, along with work ethic. These were mentioned twice as much as other phrases.

I have found from my work in showbiz, as well as every other sector, that this combo is highly effective. Many people with a strong work ethic also have a robust sense of humour. It's a combination that is unbeatable.

Dr Bell agrees: 'Those who can combine a strong work ethic and sense of humour may have the leading edge in their organizations.'

Humour helps us be 'us'

Humour creates a sense of who 'we' are, together. It's unifying. Eric Romero and Anthony Pescosolido (University of New Hampshire) found that humour helps to sustain group cohesion because it's about:

Who we are
What we are doing
How we do things

Professor Pescosolido says humour creates a 'psychological safety' which enhances attentiveness, persuasiveness and willingness to go for goals. Does that happen in your organisation?

When I find the 'wrong' sort of humour (which demeans others) in a team, it is a reflection of mutual distrust. I find it hard not to assume a great deal about a team from the nature of the ribbing or what makes people laugh in a group... or if they are not laughing together.

You may know someone who sits at the back and makes jokes or pokes fun at any new ideas or outsiders. Don't be put off by that picture. Ask you yourself: can real humour be part of the fabric of your day-to-day interactions?

I see a lot of workplaces that have a rigorous regime to check that the toilets are kept clean or have 'wellbeing initiatives' suggesting we eat our five-a-day or exercise but how many organisations make a conscious effort to keep their people and culture healthy by laughing enough each day? Laughter has plenty of beneficial physiological effects, as well as the more obvious cognitive and emotional benefits.[2]

> 'You can't laugh and be afraid at the same time.'
> Stephen Colbert

Should you recruit for humour?

Should you not hire someone who appears to lack a sense of humour? This is tricky. I certainly cannot help finding myself unconsciously 'testing' others with a moment of irony. Do they get it? We use humour for a short-hand:

Would they be enjoyable to work with?

How could they cope with the tough times?

If they don't get this, would they get my ideas, would they get me?

Once someone has laughed they will listen more readily. The conversation can be more playful, more experimental, and more open to possibilities. You may be able to make a point or criticism more humanely through humour. Though beware the cutting remark that sometimes intrudes where a gentler admonishment or suggestion would have worked better.

Humour is a great way of reducing hierarchy and unease about status. Leaders who show humour are more approachable. Humour grabs people's attention. Laughing with someone creates a bond that can see you through collaborative projects and the tough times that may lie ahead. Humour shows flexibility, an ability to see a situation from more than one side, to process it better.

Self-deprecating humour isn't just a good leadership tool but can help in negotiations, selling, sharing the limelight, or making others feel more at ease with you. We do know the difference between that and self-defeating humour.

> 'A person without a sense of humour is like a wagon without springs – jolted by every pebble in the road.'
> Henry Ward Beecher

But what if I am not funny?

Trying and failing to be funny is dreadful. Don't think you have to suddenly become class clown or dress up as Lady Gaga for the next Comic Relief Day. Let humour in. Acknowledge that it has a place at work. Look at people who can create real, spontaneous laughter. Don't stifle them.

Lightening the atmosphere at work could involve just a small comment here or there. Or just smiling and laughing with others. Make an effort to be with people in the places and at the times they laugh, not just the pub on a Friday night (there are plenty of good reasons why many will not be there then). This is as much about being seen to be laughing alongside others as being the one to create the laughter.

Can I be taught to be funny? Yes.

Not like Billy Connolly or Dawn French. But just in a gentle way. The easiest thing is just listen and remember what people say.

Very often it is no more complicated than Listen and Link. Remember what people say, and mention it later, perhaps in an unrelated scenario. That is often what great stand-ups do. We call it reincorporation, call-back or nesting and looping. They are just observing, noticing and throwing in a thought or reference from before. Remember Eddie Izzard and Mrs Badcrumble? Incongruity is an engine of humour.

It's a simple way of showing you were listening and creating a smile with not too many words. Try it today.

> 'Anyone who takes himself too seriously runs the risk of looking ridiculous; anyone who can consistently laugh at himself does not.'
> Vaclav Havel

Why smile?

If you don't smile it can make you appear nervous or unfriendly. It is hard to appear gracious if you can't smile. On the other hand, we do know when a smile is fake.

Robin Dreeke talks of 'accommodating non-verbals'. These include smiling but with your chin at a lower angle, not 'head-on' and slightly turned away. A small head tilt shows you are comfortable with the other person. A high chin angle can look aloof.

There is research into smiles, notably by Guillaume Duchenne in the nineteenth century. What we now call a Duchenne smile is genuine. A Pan Am smile is forced and is also known as the Botox smile, because that reduces the use of the small muscles around the eye. Duchenne found that a real smile involves the orbicularis oculi muscle (which causes crow's feet and raises the cheeks).

There has been plenty of research into smiling that moves it beyond just a superficial truism. Dr Paula Niedenthal, now at the University of Wisconsin, says that we can tell what is real and what is fake. We look at the geometry of the face and the situation but the main thing is we actually mimic the smile to sense whether it's fake or not. A real smile, when mimicked, activates the same areas as the other person.

Really? To make sure, she asked students to put a pencil between their lips, which engages muscles that would normally produce a smile. Because they could not mimic the smiles they saw they found it much harder to tell whether they were fake or not.

I have read that smiles have different meanings in different cultures. I know some find that we in the West smile too much. So tread carefully. I am aware that my perspective is particular to my society. 'We don't smile half as much as you do', said a Russian to my friend, Gillian King (a great communication coach) who has directed plays there.

It may sound strange but do practise your smile. How do you get it right? A slow onset smile works better, accompanied by a head tilt. This is advice from *The Journal of Non-Verbal Behaviour*. (I wonder if their editorial meetings could be a little tense.) The article is called 'Temporal Aspects of Facial Displays in Person and Expression Perception: The Effects of Smile Dynamics, Head-tilt and Gender'. We don't need to have a long clever title to know that a smile which is too quick to appear or drop away is seen as inauthentic. Or that a boy is easily encouraged by the merest of smiles from a girl.

For Dale Carnegie, smiling is principle number two of six in his pecking order. Smiling is contagious. Remember mirror neurons? When somebody smiles at us, these guys deep in our brain do a little smile of their own. That's why more than half of smiles are returned. Those feel-good neurotransmitters are released when we smile.

Feel good feedback

There is research that says not only do we smile if we are happy but if we smile we become happy.[3] It's a 'feedback loop', says Michael Lewis of the University of Cardiff: 'Emotions are not restricted to our brains. There are parts of our bodies that help and reinforce the feelings we are having.'

The brain likes smiling just as it likes exercise or chocolate. But with smiling, the brain feels good, gets our face to smile, which then tells our brain that it feels good.

Charles Darwin (yes him) developed a Facial Feedback Response Theory in 1896, suggesting that the very act of smiling makes us feel better. In a 2008 study at Echnische Universitat in Munich, involving Botox and fMRI scans, they found that imitating a smile changes what is going on in the brain. The emotional circuitry is activated when we smile.

Are you thinking, 'But I'm just not that good a smiler!' or 'people will think I am very odd if I smile all the time!' Fair enough. I sometimes have to advise people to smile less (or, more usually, not to giggle). It may affect their perceived gravitas in, say, a pitch or presentation. The giggle could well be a sign of nerves. Each situation will call you to manage yourself in different ways.

In an article in *Behavioural and Brain Sciences* in 2009, they found that 'smiling reflects different emotions in men and women'. In women, smiling signals warmth and trustworthiness, which attracts fewer, but more intimate relationships. In men, smiling signals confidence and lack of self-doubt, which attracts less intimate but more relationships.

The report's authors were Simine Vazaire, Laura Paige Naumann, Peter Renfrow and Samuel Gosling. I mention them because this research worried me. Not just because it seems to confirm some stereotypes but also because I have been telling women and men to smile in my workshops. What have I done? Often I am battling against those stereotypical views and want women to be seen as having less self-doubt. I want men to signal warmth.

Should I be telling female leaders not to smile, like some schoolteachers (male and female) say, 'Don't smile before Christmas' and 'you can soften later but you can't toughen'? As far as I can tell, the research above involved looking only at pictures of strangers faces, so are things more complex?

Lisa Feldman Barrett at Northeastern University suggests that the face doesn't tell the whole story.[4] We look at the context, body language, vocal tone and social setting. The psychologist Hillel Aviezer grafted together face and body photos from people portraying different emotions.[5] Guess what? The 'body emotion' trumped the facial one.

However effective a smile might be, there is something deeper at play. All the more reason to be aware of your body and 'lighten' it.

Lighten your body

Posture can influence the way others see you and the way you feel. Researchers have found that keeping your shoulders open and arms wide activates your hormone system in a way that makes you both feel and look more confident and capable. Please do watch Amy Cuddy's Power Pose TED Talk.

Think about the way you sit. If you're scrunched over your laptop, you won't feel very bold, but if you're sitting at a large desk, you'll feel more assertive. Hunching over a small device achieves the opposite, as well as being bad for your physique.

There is even a phenomenon now, known as Text Neck.[6] You see people everywhere looking down at their phone, bending their neck forward. It's very bad for the cervical spine. Apparently, it's the same as carrying the weight of a seven-year-old. So look down with your eyes and remember to do some neck and shoulder exercises.

A study in 2009 by Richard Petty, Pablo Brinol and Benjamin Wagner of Ohio State University found that your sitting posture affected how sure you felt of your opinions. If you sit upright, you are more convinced by your own thoughts. If you slouch you are less confident of them.

'People assume their confidence is coming from their own thoughts. They don't realise their posture is affecting how much they believe in what they're thinking,' he said. His study in 2003 found that nodding as you think made you feel more confident than if you shook your head.

Joan Meyers-Levy from the University of Minnesota found that the height of the room affects how your mind works. A higher ceiling leads to thinking more freely, more abstractly. A lower ceiling means you are more likely to focus on specifics. Do you ever think about where you meet and the type of environment relevant to the purpose of the meeting? Think of John Cleese's Open and Closed Modes.

Too often people are squeezed into small, airless, windowless rooms around a board table, hunching over laptops. Then leaders complain of a lack of innovative thinking.

Go for a walk together if you want a creative conversation.

Erik Peper is a Dutch behavioural scientist from San Francisco who has looked at posture, slumped and upright, and its effect on re-calling positive and negative thoughts. It's much easier to come up with negative thoughts when slumped (and actually rather hard to do so when upright). When upright, we do find it easier to generate positive thoughts. The way we walk affects our energy similarly.

Look upwards.

This all ties in with Amy Cuddy's work where posture is shown to affect cortisol and testosterone. The best combo is high testosterone and low cortisol. This combination, when found in people and other animals, is related to resistance to disease and leadership abilities.

From a health point of view, the best posture, no matter how good your office chair (or ball), is the one you don't keep for too long.

Simple Steps

- Practise smiling.
- Do a 'laughter audit' in your work environment.
- Laugh with other people.
- Find reasons to recall shared moments that made everyone laugh.
- Keep your posture open and upright.
- Walk, stretch and move often.

STEP SEVEN
LEAVE WELL

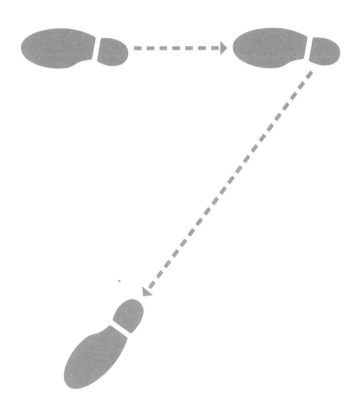

If you leave me now

We don't think enough about how we leave encounters, do we? Have any of these happened to you?

A presentation falls flat right at the last moment.

A great chat with someone you've just met ends on a jarring note.

A meeting peters out as people drift away, leaving you feeling a bit empty.

I first thought of Leave in connection with finishing a presentation. They can fizzle out or the speaker shuffles off after saying, 'Well, if there are no more questions, I'll go'. That weak last image is damaging and infects the memory of the whole piece.

Bad endings can colour your view of a whole encounter or a whole presentation. I know (from watching stand-up comics on the same bill as the sketch double-acts I did with Mike Myers and Nick Hancock in my twenties) that finishing on a high really does alter an audience's perception.[1] We always had guaranteed crowd-pleasing endings. That gave us a confidence throughout the rest of our set. (And our openings were energetic, leaving no room for doubt that we were to own the space for those twenty minutes or so).

Many stand-ups finish on their best joke, or their second best joke, if they'd used the best one as their opener.

Why are endings so important?

In a TED Talk from 2010, Daniel Kahneman talks about the difference between experience and memory.[2] How we remember something is based on two things:

The Peak: the most intense moment (good or bad)

The End: how it finished

Remember the peak-end rule.

When we recall an experience, we take an average of those two moments, not the whole. If you can combine the peak and the end, so much the better. No wonder so many performers, comics, magicians, singers (and motivational speakers, of course), look to close with an absolute belter.

In addition to this, Kahneman says we have two selves:
1. The Experiencing Self
2. The Remembering Self

Think of two different people with differing operating styles. Senor Experiencio lives moment by moment (and Kahneman thinks a moment is about three seconds). Senor Rememberio makes sense of the whole story that is later logged in our memory banks. Stories have changes, significant moments and endings. It is this self that takes any subsequent decision based on that experience.

You could say Senor Rememberio tyrannises Senor Experiencio by making him undergo experiences he may not enjoy but in hindsight can be recalled with pleasure. Thus we go on vacation, go on the scary roller-coaster or sit through a concert, just to have more memories. Kahneman uses holidays as an example. A two-week holiday isn't remembered as being twice as good as one week, is it?

He did experiments with people putting their hands in very cold water and with people having a colonoscopy. It turns out that people who had a more pleasant end experience (the final dip in the water was warmer or colon thing wasn't jiggled about as much) had a better memory of it, even though they actually spent more time in pain overall.

This is called Duration Neglect. We tend not to recall how long something was, just The Peak and The End.

To some extent, this makes sense. When there is a lot to recall, we take a snapshot or two of an experience. No use filing away the whole movie (mp4) when you can just put a couple of selfies in your mental Dropbox. The brain uses up a great deal of energy as I said before. Why should it bother remembering the whole lot?

We remember how things end disproportionately. So take advantage.

A neat handover

Do you ever feel stuck at a party or networking event? You've met someone with whom you've had a good chat. You've found things in common. You've done all the right things... learning, looking, listening, linking, letting and plenty of lightening.

However, you reach a point when you both know that the encounter is over, for now at least. You want to move on but neither of you dare. What do you do? Does one of you offer to fill up the other's glass? Or do you pretend you have to go to the toilet?

In 2010 I shared the platform with a great speaker and coach called Kate Atkin. She talked about networking and gave some brilliant advice for how to move on. Don't leave the other person high and dry as you escape to talk to another 'target'. Be honest. Say that you've enjoyed meeting him/her but that there are lots of other people present that you are hoping to meet. Then, look around the room and take her/him to meet someone else. Introduce each person to the other, then tell them something they have in common.

Maybe you don't know the new person. So introduce the person you've just met and give them the chance to open things up.

'This is Phillip. He's just been talking about his chilled distribution business. Did you know you shouldn't keep lettuce too cold?'

And off you go. You can move and Phil can talk supply chains or whatever.

> 'The other person should walk away feeling much better for having met you.'
> Dr Robin Dreeke

Follow-up

Leaving well doesn't finish there. Send an email saying how much you enjoyed meeting them or connect on LinkedIn. Even better, send something that is useful to them and shows you recall the conversation specific to that person. Giving something personalised is always effective. You could just send an email with something along the lines of ...

Here's a link to that concept we were discussing ...

Here's that article that sheds some light on ...

Yes, I did go for that five-mile run, inspired by you ...

Here are the lyrics to the Rick Astley song we couldn't recall last night ...

I'm e-introducing you to Bianca, who's looking for a distributor for her lettuce ...

How to end a meeting

One senior leader admitted that she never even thought about how to end a meeting. She worked hard at beginnings and felt she was good at them but the importance of how things were left at the end had evaded her.

Take care to ensure your meetings end well.

What is the after-taste as people head down the corridor? Here are some examples of what people might be thinking...

What a waste of time!

None of what we agreed will ever get done.

Why didn't the chair tell so-and-so to shut up?

I'll bring sandwiches next time.

We could have achieved the same in three minutes as we did in three hours.

I hope I impressed the boss with my question on KPIs.

I'm going to book my holiday now... to coincide with the next meeting.

I can't remember anything at all from this meeting.

There's been a lot happening in the car park where I've been gazing most of the time.

I dodged a bullet when I got Nick to agree to do that difficult spreadsheet.

Why didn't anyone say no when we agreed to start that stupid project?

Of course, for meetings, the end may be in the beginning. To end well, they have to start well.

Is there anything wrong with the chairperson talking to everyone individually ahead of time? Or even planning what they are going to say ahead of it? Or at least making notes during the meeting of how they will round things off?

Simple Steps for chairing meetings[3]
1. Wrap-up

Keep to the planned start and finish times. Seven minutes before the meeting is due to end (if, say, it's an hour or more), summarise where you are, invite some unheard voices to speak up or give them the opportunity to send you an email later. If somebody quiet does pipe up, give him or her the floor, without interruption. Maybe some things will have to wait for another occasion. Address those points.

As you go through the agenda, do a mini summary at the end of each topic. Beware the brooding which means that, as you are trying to deal with item ten, suddenly someone hijacks the discussion and hauls it back to item one.

Maybe you might even be able to finish the meeting early. Wouldn't that be great? Then people can be on time for their next session. (I read that Anna Wintour, the famous editor of *Vogue*, kept her meetings short. Often less than seven minutes. And they often started before the scheduled time).

2. Find the positive

Surely something good came out of it, even if it's only one thing? The more attention we pay to the upside, the more it will emerge and the greater the energy. Mention specifically the things you personally will be taking away with you. Maybe even cite an individual's contribution at a particular moment that helped moved things on significantly.

3. Deal with the elephant

The atmosphere could become a little heated. Acknowledge that. Recognise some people might be feeling a little bruised. Be thinking of ways to avoid the same issue coming up in the same way next time and leading to the same conflict.

4. Final moments

Go round the room and check which actions will be undertaken and by whom (and by when). It is more powerful if people articulate what they are going to do, rather than you. Does their body language indicate they will actually do what they say?

Stand up and gather your notes to show that the formal part of the meeting is over. Smile and ensure you manage at least a moment of eye contact with every person. Maybe that will inform who you should grab a moment with now or later, to clarify or reassure or just chat about non-work things. People should leave with the right energy to look forward to the next meeting. Maybe even organise when that is going to be, to save endless emails and poor PAs having to go back and forth with those irritating digital invites.

Be sensitive to the post-meeting vibe and see if anyone is departing in a huff.

How about one-on-ones?

When I was learning coaching at Ashridge Business School I was particularly taken by the power of summarising. It started with listening and linking. This is useful in meetings but also in conversations and mentoring.

How we ended the coaching session was really effective. The client found it helpful to hear their thoughts replayed and would often, as a result, suggest a course of action for themselves that seemed possible and positive.

Summarising at the end of conversations…
… demonstrates that you were listening
… helps you and others remember what was said
… means any promised actions are more likely to be followed through

I have worked with a brilliant company called The Right Conversation.[4] They have identified how important conversation is to every leader in every organisation. Their research has led them to identify five leadership Superskills, one of which is Flow Control. Isn't it annoying when someone keeps talking after you feel your chat is over? Or wanders off just as you're getting to the bit you think is most meaty?

Conversations have a structure. There is a beginning, a middle, and an end. Having a sense of where you are in a conversation really is a Superskill. Not taking forever, yet making the other person not feel rushed and knowing when the moment is right to bring things to an end is useful, showing both assertiveness and sensitivity.

Leaving your job

I heard a story of a CEO who left in less than amicable circumstances. He was asked to give back his company iPad. He returned it, but with the screen smashed.

That's not the best way to leave. Not only will his bosses and former colleagues think ill of him but everyone who hears the story will have their doubts too. He may have been very badly treated but all I know is that he destroyed a defenceless device.

How likely is it that you will never see any of your former colleagues or clients again? Um, NOT.

You may find yourself applying for a job with one of them one day, or they may re-emerge as a client, another speaker at an event, a consultant, a presence at a networking function or even your next-door neighbour. Or someone they know may well be one of the above. Do you really want to be known as Mr I-smashed-the-iPad?

As Herminia Ibarra has identified, it's not just who you know but who they know that matters. You have a primary network, the people you know. But your secondary network (the people that the people who you know, know) could be really useful. Or dangerous if word spreads of your blunder.

So when leaving a job, it seems simple courtesy to say thank you to those who have put up with you. They've worked hard alongside you.

Selling

Another useful time to leave well is when selling. At some point, stop talking. If you go on after you've already convinced your customer, you might lose the sale. Or when you state your fee, leave it there. Don't start immediately doing yourself down, as one of my clients admitted she found herself doing.

Pitches and presentations peter out?

Don't let your pitches end with you being subtly arm-wrestled out of the door by your prospective client. Or the gentler equivalent, when they look at their watch and cough before, 'Well, um … thanks very much. That's marvellous. We've got lots of people to see'.

You should keep your eye on the time. Finish early if you can. You need to rehearse so that you know how long your presentation is. If it's a pitch, it will be looser but you still want to end strongly. So round it off, just a few minutes ahead of time, with a neat summary of your position, one or two points and (as my investment banker friend would say), 'ask for the trade'. Make sure they know that you really want the gig, that you're not just going through the motions.

Leave the stage well. It may not be an actual stage but the enduring image of shuffling off meekly may not be the one you'd really want.

As soon as you're gone, the audience's attention will be taken elsewhere. I used to say that an audience will remember only three main points. Then a well-known presentation coach said you should make only one point. Maybe so, but you should be able to summarise your point in one sentence, or one image or one piece of data. Or a prop you hold up or give to each member of the audience.

As you deliver your killer closing line, don't look down at your notes and mumble. Learn it so that you can deliver it with verve.

It works really well if your closing has some connection with your opening. Rounding things off and tying up threads is delightful for an audience and makes it hard for them to forget your message.

I saw a great TED Talk by Pixar writer-director Andrew Stanton talking about story.[5] His credits include *Toy Story*, *Wall-E* and *Finding Nemo*. One of his great suggestions was to make the audience work a bit. They are more engaged (and will remember better) if they've had to make a mental link themselves. He summarised it as, 'Give the audience two plus two; don't give them four'. It's when they are 'a step ahead of you' and fill in the blank so you don't have to.

Then a well-known presentation coach said you should make only one point. It might be a rhetorical question or a reincorporation/call-back (that's a delayed link)...

Who do you think was sitting on the other side of the negotiating table? But this time with a very much intact iPad?
   ... Yes, you guessed it!

I needed something freezing cold but close to hand. What could I use?
   ... Finally those frozen peas came good.

I just couldn't remember her name at this networking event, then I caught site of her badge.
   ... Anyway, Mrs Badcrumble, let me introduce you to Neville. He likes cheese as well.

Be clear in your mind what you are asking of your audience as you leave. Paul McGee (a wonderful speaker and writer who also runs SUMO) says you should know what your audience are going to know, feel and do as a result of your presentation.[6]

Leaving well means keeping to time. Don't let that red light have to go into flashing mode or make the chairperson have to saunter over and rugby tackle you from the lectern. Nobody ever heckled a speaker with, 'Hey that was too short!'

I reckon most speeches should not be longer than an episode of *Neighbours*. So think twenty minutes maximum.

Look at the audience. Accept their applause. Don't rush away like a frightened mouse or as if you've encountered a nasty smell.

Leave your desk

This is another angle on Leave. Leaving your desk is such a good idea in so many ways. It's better for your posture, creativity and for making connections with other people.

Shana Lebowitz wrote about this in a blog for *Business Insider* from September 2016 entitled, 'I ditched my standing desk after nearly three months, but I took away a lesson that still makes me more productive'. She quotes Ron Freidman's book, *The Best Place to Work* and lists good reasons why you shouldn't be stuck at your desk all day. Moving around gives you energy, lifts your heart rate, and keeps your blood flowing.

It's also a good idea to go somewhere else to do a specific task. At your desk you might try and multi-task which, by the way, is a myth. You cannot multi-task. You just end up starting multiple tasks and not doing any of them well.

Multi-tasking = Multi-flailing

That place you move to concentrate could be a café (even better if you turn off the Wi-Fi, in my experience). Make yourself focus on one thing while you are in that one place.

Friedman says that changing environment is best for a task that requires deep thinking, focused concentration or learning new information, or for something you don't particularly enjoy. That won't be everything you do, but removing yourself from your normal place could really help you complete a finicky job.

Simple Steps

- Think specifically (in advance) about endings.

- Follow up with the people you meet, send a helpful email or just a short note.

- Rehearse the final line of your presentation so you can deliver it with verve.

- Find new environments for specific tasks.

I'm leaving now

When I presented a session on the Seven Ls at the London Business Forum, a very good friend came to watch. Like any good friend, without me asking, he told me exactly what he thought. He observed that I did not leave well, despite this being my advice to the audience. Ouch. That's what friends are for.

So I want to leave well now, as we say goodbye, dear reader. The more I have helped people with communication skills, the more I have realised that the best question I can ask is, 'So what?' You may have charisma (which anybody can learn) but do you have a story to tell? Is there purpose in your organisation beyond its existence?

'We have forgotten that organisations are first and foremost places of human interaction, not just transaction.'
Dr Emma Seppala

My method of teaching presentation skills is to ask people to pre-pare their piece. Then, when they arrive, I tell them to put that to one side. 'Tell me in your own, semi-improvised words', I ask. Then something happens. They become confident in their words, rather than fearful of forgetting their lines.

So do practise these people skills. The more you do them, the more you will want to do them. But you need to care about your job. There is so much research on the importance of purpose. And do you know the other thing that gives us meaning?

Gratitude

Simply writing down or talking or thinking about what you have to be grateful for begins to make you notice more. Don't wait until you leave your job to remember the things you would miss if you left.

Leave your day well
You don't have to do very much. Just at the end of the day, think of three things for which you are grateful. We know the phrase,

'Count your blessings' but many ancient cultures recognise the importance of acceptance.

One of the many wonderful stories featuring the ancient Persian folk character, Mullah Nasruddin, has him advising a man who felt his house was too small. The Mullah told him to bring his chickens into his house. Then some more of his animals the next day, and so on for a week. Then he told him to put the animals back out in the yard.

Once the animals were out, the man was delighted. His house felt bigger now. This pre-figures the psychological phenomenon of Hedonic Adaptation, which means we easily become used to our level of comfort or luxury, whatever it may be.

You've got a washing machine? You want a better one. Then a tumble dryer. Then someone to put in the clothes for you. And take them out. And iron them. And go and choose them for you. Then you want better clothes. Then you don't even want to wear clothes more than once, so why even have a washing machine?
'Take full account of the excellencies which you possess and, in gratitude, remember how you would hanker after them if you had them not', said Marcus Aurelius in Roman times, a little before washing machines were invented.

Expressing gratitude releases serotonin in the brain. That's the hormone that controls mood. Gratitude creates a perspective. You could say it produces self-fulfilling optimism. And there is plenty of other scientific evidence for the observable benefits of gratitude:
1. You will be more hopeful and healthier
2. You will sleep better

3. You will have higher self-esteem
4. You will be more helpful and empathetic
5. You will be more resilient[7]

Each of these is based on separate, specific studies but are they not of a piece? They all seem related. It may be to do with the Remembering Self. Consciously making Senor Rememberio focus on the good stuff may mean that you'll see things as generally good and that becomes self-fulfilling. So write things down as you leave the day for which you are grateful. You can use the back of the notebook I suggested you buy in Step One, Learn.

Goodbye

I have offered you advice that I found works with my clients. I hope you can introduce some Simple Steps along the way.

Notice, however, that they may not always work. You should be aware that an angry driver honking his horn as you fumble for your car park ticket will not be calmed by your attentive body language, strong eye contact and reflective questioning. Paying and getting out of the way works best here. (Though a quick mouthed 'sorry' does help a lot I find.)

It all depends on the context. You might try something and fall flat on your face. That is no reason not to try. By calling them Simple Steps I hope you've understood these are small, practical tweaks... but they can make a big difference overall.

Remember the one percent marginal gain? Are you at seven yet? Please do let me know...

ENDNOTES

Step One, Learn
1. 'The Comeback of Cursive', *The Economist*, September 2016.

Step Two, Look
1. Michael Ellsberg, *The Power of Eye Contact* (2010).
2. Paul Ekman Group, http://www.paulekman.com.
3. Frank Farrelly and Jeffrey M. Brandsma, *Provocative Therapy* (1989).
4. Samuel McNerney, 'A Brief Guide to Embodied Cognition: Why You Are Not Your Brain', *Scientific American*, 4 November 2011, https://blogs.scientificamerican.com/guest-blog/a-brief-guide-to-embodied-cognition-why-you-are-not-your-brain.
5. Dr Rizzolati, an Italian neurophysiologist and professor at the University of Parma in Italy, discovered unique neurons in the frontal and premotor cortex which he called mirror neurons.

Step Three, Listen
1. Seth S. Horovitz, 'The Science and Art of Listening', *New York Times*, 9 November 2012, http://www.nytimes.com/2012/11/11/opinion/sunday/why-listening-is-so-much-more-than-hearing.html.
2. The Comedy Store Players perform improv every Wednesday and Sunday in London. Come and say hello: comedystoreplayers.com.
3. From the Jo Cox maiden speech in the House of Commons, 3 June 2015. You can watch it here: https://www.parliament.uk/business/news/2016/june/jo-cox-maiden-speech-in-the-house-of-commons.
4. Jack Zenger and Joseph Folkman, 'What Great Listeners Actually Do', *Harvard Business Review*, 14 July 2016.
5. Ralph G. Nichols and Leonard A. Stevens, 'Listening to People', *Harvard Business Review*, September 1957.

6. I recommend reading the following: Charna Halpern, Del Close and Kim Howard Johnson, *Truth in Comedy: The Manual for Improvisation* (1994).

Step Four, Link

1. Robert Poynton, *Everything's An Offer: How to do more with Less*, illustrated by Gary Hirsch (2008).
2. Paul Plsek is a properly clever fellow. He led engineering teams at AT&T Bell Laboratories (telecommunications R&D) and was director of corporate quality planning at AT&T. He developed the concepts of DirectedCreativity and PatterMapping, helping organisations to be creative and innovative. He's a nice chap too.
3. Greg J Stephens, Lauren Silbert and U Hasson, 'Speaker-Listener Neural Coupling Underlies Successful Communication', *National Academy of Sciences* vol. 107, no. 32 (August 2010).
4. Elliot Aronson, *The Social Animal* (1972).
5. David H. Maister, Robert Galford and Charles Green, *The Trusted Advisor* (2000).
6. Catherine Blythe, *The Art of Conversation: A Guided Tour of a Neglected Pleasure* (2008).

Step Five, Let

1. R. I. M. Dunbar and Anna Marriott and N. D. C. Duncan, 'Human Nature', *Human Conversational Behaviour*, vol. 8, no. 3 (September 1997).
2. Daniel A. Gross, 'This is Your Brain on Silence', *Nautilus*, issue 16, 21 August 2014, http://nautil.us/issue/16/nothingness/this-is-your- brain-on-silence.

Step Six, Lighten

1. Bell Leadership Institute, March 2012, https://www.bellleadership. com/humor-gives-leaders-edge.
2. Jenna Goudreau, 'Are Funny People More Successful in Business?' *Forbes*, 21 February 2012.
3. Melinda Wenner, 'Smile! It Could Make You Happier', *Scientific American*, 1 September 2009, https://www.scientificamerican.com/

article/ smile-it-could-make-you-happier. There's some other good stuff about smiling in this article.

4. Lisa Feldman Barrett, 'What Faces Can't Tell Us', *New York Times*, 28 February 2014.

5. Hillel Aviezer, Yaacov Trope and Alexander Todorov, 'Body Cues, Not Facial Expressions, Discriminate Between Intense Positive and Negative Emotions' Science Magazine, 30 November 2012, http:// science.sciencemag.org/content/338/6111/1225.

6. Lindsey Bever, 'Text neck' is becoming an "epidemic" and could wreck your spine', *Washington Post*, 20 November 2014, https:// www.washingtonpost.com/news/morning-mix/wp/2014/11/20/ text-neck-is-becoming-an-epidemic-and-could-wreck-your-spine/?utm_term=.55e0e88d536e.

Step Seven, Leave Well

1. If you really want to see me in my youthful double-acts: http://all-thatmullarkey.com/doubleacts.html.

2. Daniel Kahneman, 'The Riddle of Experience vs. Memory', TED Talk, February 2010, https://www.ted.com/talks/daniel_kahneman_the_riddle_of_experience_vs_memory.

3. I found the following blogs helpful on this matter:
    - Paul Axtell, 'The Right Way to End a Meeting', *Harvard Business Review*, 11 March 2015.
    - Peter Economy, '7 Ways to End Every Meeting on a Positive Note', *Inc.com*, 19 May 2016.
    - Susan Adams, 'How To Run a Meeting', *Forbes*, 5 October 2015.

4. The Right Conversation, therightconversation.co.uk.

5. Andrew Stanton, 'The clues to a great story', *TED Talk*, February 2012, https://www.ted.com/talks/andrew_stanton_the_clues_to_a_great_story.

6. Paul McGee and his great training company: http://www.thesumo guy.com.

7. Douglas Main, 'Five Scientifically Proven Benefits of Gratitude', *Newsweek*, 25 November 2015.

FURTHER READING

Caroline Goyder, *Gravitas* (2014).
Dale Carnegie, *How to Win Friends and Influence People* (1936).
Daniel Kahneman *Thinking Fast and Slow* (2011).
Herminia Ibarra, *Act Like a Leader, Think Like a Leader* (2015).
Robin Dreeke, *It's Not All About Me* (2013).
Steven Covey, *The Seven Habits of Highly Effective People* (1989).

About Neil Mullarkey

Neil Mullarkey co-founded London's *Comedy Store Players*, Europe's top improvisation ensemble, in 1985, and still performs with them. He has acted on TV, radio and in two *Austin Powers* films with his former comedy partner, Mike Myers.

Nowadays his communication and creative expertise is in demand across the world. He has worked in 23 countries with clients including Google, Microsoft, Saatchi & Saatchi, Barclays, Vodafone, EY, Deloitte and Unilever. He is a regular speaker at the London Business Forum and a visiting lecturer at Cass Business School, City University of London.

www.neilmullarkey.com
🐦 @neilmullarkey

About London Business Forum

Founded in 2002, London Business Forum offers a programme of fun and insightful events presented by some of the world's most inspiring people.

London Business Forum also create uplifting books filled with ideas and insights for professional and personal development. If you would like to buy London Business Forum publications for your organisation, or just have a chat, contact them at:

www.londonbusinessforum.com
info@londonbusinessforum.com
+44 (0)20 7600 4222
🐦 @LBFEvents